Leadership from the Foundation Up

Reflections to Guide Your Leadership Journey

Glenn Robertson

with
Kaleigh Kanary

Leadership from the Foundation Up: Reflections to Guide Your Leadership Journey

Pencil on Paper
www.pencilonpaper.ca

ISBN 978-1-7382408-3-8 (paperback)

ISBN 978-1-7382408-2-1 (ebook)

ISBN 978-1-7382408-1-4 (audiobook)

Cover design by Shane Kroetsch, Fatima Kamal, and Deb Lawton

Contents

What You Will Come To Understand

Dedication

This book is dedicated to my eldest daughter, Kaleigh Kanary. She was an integral part of its development, layout, and editing. Kaleigh had a unique talent, developed during childhood, of helping me get to the point succinctly, and she gave me great advice to present my stories here in the best light possible. While writing this together, she often told me, "I'm going to beat the Maritimer out of you yet". In other words, Kaleigh helped me weave a tale and still be coherent. My greatest joy in writing this book was when we were working on it together. I can see her direction, voice, and love in these words and can visualize her many ringed coffee stains exchanged throughout various edits of this book. Kaleigh tragically passed away on August 11, 2023, as we were working toward editing the final pages. Helping to create and publish this book is a small part of her legacy, but a loving reminder of who she was to our family and how talented she was. Our hearts will forever miss her.

Reflections from Retirement

Well, it's the first Monday morning of my retirement, and I am officially off the clock, not that I ever felt I was on one. My retirement announcement came early, nine months before my official date, which made time crawl for me and those around me. It was necessary, though, as it allowed my leadership team and successor enough runway to prepare, and more than enough time to say goodbye.

I had many people I wanted to thank—leaders, mentors, colleagues, customers, and vendors. There were lots of last dinners, meetings, and calls to say goodbye. I decided to post my departure on LinkedIn a couple days before my official date. The responses were overwhelming. Hundreds of people I had not seen or spoken with for years, right back to my very first company, reached out to wish me well. To say the comments were heartwarming would understate the kindness shown. The experience was emotional, and it hit me at the core.

During this time, I reflected back to my very first leadership roles and how young and inexperienced I was—

some of the decisions that were taken, the mistakes I often made, and the learning I had. I contemplated how my career started and quickly led to a leadership role, then another, and another. Many people may ask the question during their career, why me? Well, why not? Through working with primary producers of seafood and agriculture, retail and food service distributors, group purchasing organizations, and several years of owning and operating restaurants, I have experienced the entire lifecycle of the food industry. So many business meetings, hotel rooms, miles traveled, and decisions made. It has been a long and winding road, and for me, it's over.

My style has always been to share stories to help illustrate a point. Storytelling is a valuable way for organizations to bridge past employees with current and new. As such, you will find short tales in this book that took place over my extensive leadership career, which took me across Canada and the globe. Starting from humble roots and working up to senior executive roles has given me a unique lens to view all facets of an organization. This perspective proves that leadership is universal, and generally, what works well in one sector or industry will do so in another. Admittedly, these stories will not fit every circumstance, but they were selected to reflect the fundamental traits that influenced my career in the most positive ways.

Here I sit, on this cold November morning, and I wonder, what has it all meant? I have a feeling there is a lot of relevant information in my head, how some of my evolution as a leader might be good to share, like how others helped me, and that I need to get it out before I start to lose some of those valued memories. So, let us go back to the beginning, where all good stories start.

I hope this book will inspire you, provide key insights, and some wisdom as you work on your own journey— whether you are in your first leadership role, or are a seasoned leader seeking a new point of view. May your path through leadership be just as enjoyable and rewarding as mine.

Glenn

Leadership from the Foundation Up

Reflections to Guide Your Leadership Journey

Glenn Robertson

with
Kaleigh Kanary

Finding Your Way

Chapter 1

Answering the Call
Origins of a Leader

I did not show much promise in early childhood. I had no desire to be a straight-A student and did not study very hard. My report card comments reflected my efforts. *Your son is very social and could study more.* My confidence made up for what I lacked in academic interest, though I had yet to figure out what I had to offer. The truth is, I failed to see the relevance of some of the subjects taught. School did not inspire me to pursue a particular career path, so when it came to graduation time, I wondered what should come next.

My grandfather spent many years aboard the S.S. Lovat as Chief Steward and baker, looking after the crew. In my early years, he would sit me on his kitchen counter to watch him prepare pastries and pies from big bins of flour, sugar, and oats. His Enterprise wood oven wafted smoke and baking dough through the entire house and would propel me toward the kitchen first thing in the morning. It is not a coincidence that I would spend much of my career in the food industry and just as many hours of my free time cooking with my family.

My mother's family were French-speaking Acadians and

were very social, as I would turn out to be. My grandfather would welcome neighbors and friends into his kitchen and offer anyone that passed by something to eat. I can still hear the old screen door hinge creaking and the sound of the Stella Maris Church bells on Sunday mornings, calling all Pictou, Nova Scotia's sinners to account. Years after he was gone, a recording of his voice and those sounds instantly took me back to my earliest memories. I saw him just two days before he passed. He got out of his bed at the nursing home and went back to his then unoccupied house to bake a blueberry pie for us to enjoy together. It certainly highlighted the things that he held close to his heart, and I wish I appreciated it more at the time.

That same year, I had my first leadership experience when I was selected to be Captain of my minor league hockey team. This choice was not because I was noticeable leadership material. Instead, it was because I scored a few goals early in the season, and people are often selected to lead when they excel as players. Over time, it became apparent that not all good players made good leaders and vice versa.

As young as I was, the lesson that stuck with me from that experience was this: as Captain, you are addressed directly by game officials, and when you win the championship, they hand the trophy to the captain first so they can share with the team. It felt special and deep down it likely triggered a thought process in my mind that it was much more fun to be the leader than not be.

Key Takeaway

Leaders emerge through many circumstances, in families, cultural groups, religions, sports clubs, and all shapes and sizes of organizations. Any group that requires direction and contains more than one person will ultimately need someone to lead. Finding yourself subconsciously pulled into leadership could signal that you are heading on an exciting path of opportunities.

Chapter 2

Self-Awareness

Everyone Is Watching What You Say and Do

When I was fifteen, I began what turned out to be my life's career in the food business. I worked part-time in the bakery department of a large supermarket chain, likely influenced by the time spent on my grandfather's counter.

In those days, bakers did the baking from scratch, unlike today, where most products are cooked in a pre-made frozen state. I remember mixing huge vats of ingredients for cakes and pies, often carrying large sacks of flour and sugar from the storage area. My papa would have been proud of my interest in his expert craft.

Like him, our grocery store manager, Mr. Miller, was always sharply dressed. In a three-piece blue suit, he spent much of his time at the front of the store greeting customers by name, packing groceries, and being present. That kind of old-fashioned service is not something we see anymore.

One busy Saturday at Christmas time, he came to the bakery at the back of the store and encouraged us to pick up the pace on the production of apple pies. When he left, he stood on the other side of the bakery's swinging doors, his

6

back facing where we would throw garbage into a large opening in the wall. I was trying to wrangle a hefty 40kg bag of flour, about the same size as me, with a rip in the middle. Heading to the re-pack area, I swayed toward and pushed through the swinging doors as the bag split entirely in half.

The flour hit the store manager between his pocket watch and his shiny shoes. His crisp blue suit was now a fine pastry white, and his round glasses were caked in thick flour dust. I thought I was done. Yet, he went out of his way not to blame me for the incident. He could have yelled, belittled, or even fired me. I thought he might, but he started to laugh, along with a couple of others that saw it, and asked me to watch my aim the next time. Luckily, his reaction left as much of a mark on me as the flour did on him.

I learned over time that, as a leader, you are on display from the time you arrive in the parking lot until you leave at night. Others will notice your body language when you greet the people you work with. Are you smiling, or are you scowling? Do you acknowledge people with a "good morning", or are you reading an email on your phone that you think is more important? Do you walk the floor, building, or warehouse and stop to ask employees how their day is going or how their families are doing? Or do you stay in your office with your door closed? Do you actively listen in meetings, or are you already thinking of next week's long-term strategy session?

Your demeanor, body language, and words signal your mood and approachability. They will either increase the positivity in your workplace or diminish it. Being present is so important to those around you. Unfortunately, it is easy these days not to be. Technology bombards us with tools that allow us to communicate quickly and efficiently, both in our personal lives and in the corporate world. The new digital world has massive benefits, but it also has conditioned many of us to prioritize it over those in front of us. The constant need to be responding to others can send the wrong message. It can tell the people in front of you, what I am doing is more important than you are.

Your mood ebbs, rises, and falls based on what is going on in your life. I believe I am a positive person and present myself that way, so it always surprised me when someone asked if I was okay or having a bad day if I was not smiling. It reinforced that people are attuned to how you are feeling and, more importantly, how it might impact them. Body language, like your posture, how quickly or slowly you move, and how you use your hands, communicate your inner world. At the same time, how you speak, your tone, and your eyes also factor into how people interpret your mood. People watch you while you are standing away from a crowd, walking down the hall, or sitting at your desk. This may sound dramatic, but these small changes in movement, behavior, or tone will show more than you realize. Try to remain conscientious about how you appear, and act as your natural self whenever possible.

Consistency is key. Being the same person to everyone you work with is just as important. We should make the conscious effort to be the same person to everyone, no matter their background or what role they hold. Team members will notice if you treat people upstream differently than one downstream, and we all have those at both ends of the spectrum. People watch everything you do, what you say, and how you respond, so ensure you give all employees the fair time and attention they deserve.

As I think about that leader I dumped flour on years ago, I wonder, how would they have reacted today? Would they be on a cell phone, distracted from the here and now? Would they react with care and understanding? Would they have the self-awareness to see the bigger picture, or might they simply say, "you are fired"?

Key Takeaway

The way my leader positively reacted to the situation became part of the path I took. It made a difference, just like many decisions we make as leaders. This affected my view on my approachability and shaped how I reacted to issues throughout my career. Never underestimate the responsibility you have in what you do and how you show up every day. Remember, even little conversations, decisions, and reactions can have a profound impact on others.

Chapter 3

Advocates and Mentors

Surrounding Yourself with a Support Network

While I was a teenager, a door to a leadership role opened. I started to work as a minor hockey official, taking on more games than hours in the day and loving being in the rink and learning a new craft. As a minor hockey referee, you learn humanity from an entirely new lens. At the time, I did not feel prepared for the role, nor did I understand it would set me on the leadership path.

My days as a young official eventually led me to an opportunity to become Referee-in-Chief for the Shearwater East Dartmouth Minor Hockey Association, who have since developed great players such as Sydney Crosby and Nathan MacKinnon. The former Chief suddenly resigned and left the league with few options. I had a couple of part-time jobs and initially declined, as the role required shifts every night to assign officials to hundreds of games a week by phone, and I would not be able to referee as much as I wanted. The Referee-in-Chief also worked with a league executive comprised entirely of opinionated parents. That did not sound like a good time to me.

The President of the league told me it would be a great opportunity for me to work for the community and would look good on a resume. His reasoning caught my attention enough to say yes, and I'm so glad he pushed me into my first challenging leadership role. Almost every night, officials called in sick or did not show up at a rink, requiring me to spend nearly every waking minute outside of school at the arena. My experience overseeing players older than me and the responsibility of being Referee-in-Chief provided some of the best lessons in leadership and in life. It also gave me an avenue to give back to my community. I volunteered with the Canadian National Institute for the Blind, which organized games for kids with vision loss. What a genuinely humbling opportunity to work with kids with more significant challenges than I had.

From early leadership positions like these, young people can learn the importance of diplomacy, patience, and confidence in making difficult decisions. I certainly had to figure out how to ignore unconstructive comments and even abuse, often being called every possible hurtful adjective. Most of the time, rude or ignorant comments were merely background noise. As an official, you learn to ignore it and focus on what is in front of you, not what is behind you. Regrettably, most kids who try officiating any sport drop out in the first year. It is an unfortunate statistic, since getting into sports at any level is an incredible way to learn life lessons. Whether an individual participates as a player, coach, or especially as an official, leadership qualities can shine if supported.

Over time, it was clear that not all decisions I made as an official were the right ones. I admit I blew more than a few calls. Even so, I learned from my mistakes. I received solid advice on one of my many journeys to a pre-season conditioning camp, hosted by National Hockey League Referee, Bruce Hood, known to be the best official of the time. When he came to pick me up after a late-night train arrival in Toronto, I asked him what made him a top NHL referee. To this day, I still remember some of those suggestions:

- Be 100% prepared. There are no shortcuts.
- Be confident about your decisions without being arrogant.
- Grow from constructive criticism and accept your mistakes. There will be lots of them.

I had yet to learn that those principles would be as foundational to my business leadership as they were for being a great official. If we stop and think about it, the variety of activities we do every day cross over and provide opportunities for us to learn. Our brains are wired to use new information and put it into practice. In our younger years, many do not believe they are destined to be leaders or make deliberate decisions to get there. Yet, many roles we seek are just that. Teachers are a great example of what leadership can be all about. They guide, teach, support, and help us through our formative developmental years. When reflecting on your childhood, you may think of a teacher or two who had a positive impact on you and shaped some of who you are.

Leadership requires unique skills, and who does it well is apparent. As you start your career and throughout your journey, be purposeful in surrounding yourself with people who do it well and take an interest in your development. If you are open to it, some of their brilliance will rub off on you.

We all need someone to believe in us, take a chance on us, offer guidance, or present us with an opportunity that will lead to our growth. I didn't understand what the word mentor meant when I asked for advice in that car all those years ago, but I was fortunate enough to have leaders and friends to offer me advice. Professional or not, these relationships can provide a meaningful form of mentorship. I was so happy to have three of those individuals sitting with me at my eldest daughter's wedding. During the night, I took the chance to tell them about the positive impact they had on my growth and success as a leader.

One mentor was a former owner of a large distribution company in Western Canada. After an acquisition, I came to work with him prior to his retirement as part of a new Canadian senior leadership team. He understood the distribution industry inside and out and had as sharp a business mind as I have ever seen. He was an excellent leader to emulate. His style was calm and extremely candid, but with a dry sense of humor. This mentor would often show me that no matter what the issue was, remaining calm and pragmatic in your approach could create stability for those around you.

The second mentor was a former customer who became a close, lifelong friend. He ran an award-winning business in Yorkshire, England, and was successfully self-made and highly entrepreneurial. Over the past 30 years, we spent a lot of time fly-fishing together in Scotland, which provided time to relax, and to consider philosophies on life and business. He was a consummate debater, often taking an adversarial stance on issues. We would argue and laugh until it was time to get up and go fishing. He made me stronger in business.

The third was a close childhood friend who is well educated and worked outside my industry. He is an incredible listener, and I feel grounded during our conversations. Having people in your life who are good listeners demonstrates the value of being in the moment. It is truly a gift to have someone willing to just be there for you when you need them.

These types of relationships can give you a different perspective to inform your thoughts and decisions. The key to growth and success as a leader is to ask for help and accept it when it is offered.

So how, as a young leader, do you look for or start to form mentor relationships? First, you can ask your company if any formal programs exist or if there's an opportunity to start one. Ask your leader if you can meet with senior executives, supervisors, or coworkers who may help expand your knowledge base and network. It can be helpful to have at least one internal mentorship, as they can be a strong advocate for you in your current role and provide guidance for the future. For more formal programs where mentors are selected for you, the key is chemistry and trust. It may take time to establish a deeper relationship—however, it's worth the effort. Both mentor and mentee need to make a genuine commitment for the process to work effectively.

Look outside your organization for mentorship. Try people you know and respect from different walks of life, different industries, or retired leaders who may have experiences to share. It can all start with a phone call, an in-person exchange where you ask the person to give you time, a coffee break, or an after-work beer. People are usually very flattered to be approached to help, so just ask.

Once you establish a relationship, use the time wisely, and prepare questions before you meet. Discuss your approach to an issue, then ask your mentor about how they would have addressed it. Be honest about your feelings, your decisions and your failures. It will lead to deeper conversations that will ultimately lead to your growth. Remember, mentors are not a tool to solve your problems. However, they can give guidance that allows you to develop leadership skills and fine tune your approach to your decision-making process.

As your career progresses, you can lean into many of your closest business relationships and a dual mentorship could unfold. A person you see as a mentor may surprise you by telling you about a time your advice and guidance made a difference to them. In reality, mentorship will take on different forms throughout your career. Remember to share the positive impact others have had on you by thanking anyone who has acted as a mentor to you during your career. Those emails or phone calls can make a lasting impact. You will be glad you took the time to do it.

Key Takeaway

Develop a strong network of mentors and supporters early in your career. Your success is not an isolated experience. You will need other's help to achieve your potential.

Chapter 4

Overcoming Challenges
Nothing Is Impossible

Very early in my career, after a short stint as a sales representative, I was asked to relocate from Halifax, Nova Scotia, to Charlottetown, Prince Edward Island. My organization had acquired a small family-run produce company in a province that had huge seasonal business over the summer months. This move would take me away from my home but push me into leadership as General Manager.

My wife, Kathy, and I were excited and scared at the prospect of leaving the comfort of home and experiencing something new. It seems silly now but traveling a few hundred kilometers at that time felt like we were on the other side of the world.

Regrettably, a short time after the sale went through, the owner of the business we acquired had a heart attack and passed away. His passing jolted me with the reality that the person who was supposed to stay and help hand over the ropes of his business was now gone. Now without support, the prospect of taking on the role looked much more challenging and far less exciting to an inexperienced leader. Several weeks later, just prior to heading to Charlottetown to take over the business, another disaster struck —the business's building burned to the ground.

It seemed impossible that two events of this magnitude could happen so quickly. After meeting with my boss, we decided to rent or buy a facility to operate from. Luckily, within a few days, another wholesale company on the island offered us space to get started from. We cobbled together some racking, moved inventory in, and got back up and running, all with only missing a couple of days of work.

It wasn't easy to navigate the needs of this new territory. I was not an Islander, I was an outsider, or as locals called us, CFA: "Come from Away". Like many in small family-run businesses, the employees were not empowered to make important decisions. So, as their new leader, I needed to quickly figure out who I could lean on for help.

As things started to work out, one final, significant issue occurred. When my company took control of operations, we ordered a couple new trucks decaled in our new brand colors. We wanted to make a statement that we had arrived. When I sent for the first one to be picked up, our somewhat inexperienced driver decided to take a shortcut between the ferry in Borden and Charlottetown. Unknowingly, the driver selected a road with a railway tunnel crossing about twelve inches lower than the height of the truck, and he failed to read the warning when driving toward it. He hit the top of the tunnel with so much force that it peeled the top of the truck back twenty-five feet, making it look like a freshly opened sardine can. The driver was lucky not to be injured in the accident. However, the truck was not so fortunate. In order to get the truck out of the tunnel, it needed to be cut apart and then rebuilt. This situation was another setback, but we just needed to figure out how to work around it.

When I reflect on these events, the decisions I made through the ordeal happened just as quickly as the disasters. I remember thinking, "what am I getting myself into?" and "how will we ever get this business back to successful operations?". I knew this new project would take a lot of heavy lifting, and feeling confident did not come easily.

Over my career, there would be many more setbacks and challenges that, at the time, seemed like significant hurdles. These include lightning strikes, power failures, computer system crashes, labor issues, lockdowns, hurricanes, the 1998 Swiss Air Disaster (where 200 people perished within a few miles of our facility) and Y2K (when the end and beginning of a century created the need for extraordinary preparation and diligence). Even in my final years of service, we faced a global pandemic from COVID-19, fires, record-breaking floods and extreme heat waves. The lesson I learned over my career is that all issues, no matter how big they appear to be at times, are surmountable. Remember, all of us will face headwinds as leaders, and while you cannot control the wind, you can adjust your sails. In every case, when things look impossible, you need to find a horizon to work toward, and no matter how unclear things are, continue to see the positives inside of what can be very difficult days. In time, things will get better and get back to normal. Maybe a new normal, but normal nonetheless.

The dark days and the toughest issues will present the greatest opportunity for personal growth. Leadership is about initiating, being the change, and showing people how to get to the other side. While management is required to execute and keep operating, leadership is what people need while in the thick of hardship. Leaders are there to help establish or support the team's plan, recognize the requirements, and motivate everyone to head in the same direction.

Key Takeaway

During your career, you will be faced with obstacles that are completely out of your control, and that create circumstances that seem overwhelming and insurmountable. Have faith and be resolute that you will find your way. One thing is certain: if you do not have faith, no one else will.

Chapter 5

Pride and Humility
Balancing Your Emotional Self

My Maritime roots often show up in my choice of words or how I say things. Being Nova Scotian has always been something I am proud of. During the pandemic, the shocking and tragic 2020 mass shooting, which killed 22 people, occurred back home. It reminded me how much my wife and I ached for our friends, family, and the people of Nova Scotia and wished to be there to help in any way we could.

The pride I feel every time Nova Scotians show their true colors in the face of challenging odds continues to inspire me. My roots run deep. My love of our east coast music, culture, food, and generosity has influenced me to take life head-on, just like they do. When strangers were in trouble, like on September 11th, 2001, when flights were grounded and travelers were stranded and needing help, our friends and neighbors drove to the airport to help in any way they could. I loved growing up and starting my career and family there.

In my younger years, I remember hearing very prejudicial comments about Easterners, mainly from people who are not Easterners. Contrary to the stereotype that we are lazy, dumb, and looking for an unemployment check, we in fact have the highest University educated population per capita in Canada. It does not always matter where we come from, but where we come from can influence who we become.

Pride can be many things. It can show up in confidence, self-respect and esteem, dignity, and honor. It is how you represent yourself, your family, community, culture, or country. As a Canadian, it can manifest while watching Canada beat the USA in the 2010 Olympics for the gold medal in hockey.

On the other side of the blade is humility, which is often held in balance with our ego. Would our country's humility have been on display if we lost? Would we have conceded graciously and accepted the outcome we did not expect or want? The same rules apply from the ice to the office. We may not be our best selves in the heat of an epic hockey game, but we need to be when in the heat of battle at work. How you balance your ego with humility in a business setting tells a lot about the leader you wish to be.

We bring our pride of purpose and place with us to work. It is reflected in our confidence and how we carry ourselves. As leaders, we need the confidence to have strong convictions in our decision-making.

Confidence lives somewhere between pride and humility. Like the saying, "Don't get too high on the ups and too low on the lows", you have to find the balance to lead you in the right direction.

I feel proud of many things, but pride can be a double-edged sword. If you come off too sure of yourself, it can be interpreted as egotistical or cocky. When pride runs amuck, it shows up as its ugly stepsister, arrogance. If you've heard these words to describe how you function at work, you may need to show humility more often. That could mean a willingness to be open, show empathy, or uncertainty. When you see yourself at an untouchable level that can do no wrong, your behavior and attitude say you are not open to discussion, feedback, or other possibilities.

I have been there. We can all be guilty of reading our own press clippings. It's an uncomfortable feeling knowing that I not just wanted, but needed, to be right. When that happened, the outcome might have been what I sought, but it damaged relationships because I let my pride and overconfidence get the best of me.

As a leader, you want to be strong, confident, and right. You may even be projecting that image without trying. The concern then becomes, does that put you in a situation where you are no longer open to other's thoughts? Worse than that, if you force a decision due to your overconfidence and it is wrong, it reflects not only poor judgment on your part but a lack of openness. Some, even in the face of this, will double down on their opinions and decisions. Unfortunately, it compounds the problem by putting yourself in the corner with no way out.

A great leader does not let their pride and confidence override their ability to listen, understand, or support others. Some leaders really struggle with this idea. One individual from early in my career fit that bill. He was a macho-minded guy who talked very loud. His overconfidence on every issue left little to no room for the rest of us to contribute, even if we were asked. He sucked the oxygen out of the room. Looking back, this person knew their stuff and was right a lot of the time. However, because of his arrogance and dominance, he stunted the development of everyone around him. No one ever stepped in to challenge or ask tough questions because he always talked the loudest, spoke the most, and at times, on top of others trying to speak. After a while, employees gave up. While he thought he had the team's buy-in, people were checked out, gave no discretionary support, and our results suffered.

A lack of self-awareness tends to show up with bad leaders, and ultimately, they are not successful in the long run. Even when you encounter poor leadership along your journey, try to use the experience to learn what you should do differently. If the opportunity allows, provide them with feedback. It may be awkward, but you will find you can learn as much from poor leaders as from good ones.

Key Takeaway

By learning to temper your emotions and reactions as a leader, and appropriately reflecting a balanced sense of pride and humility, you will find your team's ability to adapt to and enjoy your leadership style easier, allowing them to focus on the deliverables and achieve them more consistently.

Chapter 6

Preparedness

Preparing for Anything, Including the Why

As a young hockey official, I learned the rules inside and out and prided myself in knowing and applying them during a game. That didn't stop a brawl from breaking out during the National Anthem while refereeing my first Junior A game in Prince Edward Island. The music played on, but eventually everyone tired enough for calm to return so the game could commence.

Later that night, the local CBC news reported that a newcomer referee lost control of the game. Funny, the game had to start in order to lose control. I guess I could not do much worse in people's eyes if they believed that was true.

Frankly, many things in life are out of our total control. It is difficult to be certain what will happen in any circumstance, but being prepared to the best of our ability will allow a chance for better outcomes.

As I entered business life, I believed that rules like policies and procedures are generally the same. I soon learned that running a business was far more complex than a set of rules or guidelines and preparing for business situations, such as employee relations, labor challenges, or customer issues, required a far wider range of skills than knowing basic rules or principles. However, proper preparation is the absolute entry-level requirement for anything you hope to excel at, especially leadership.

After several years of experience in diverse leadership roles, and a couple of months of working for an international exporter as their sales and distribution leader, I planned an extensive trip abroad to East Asia to meet with several of our largest customers and a few new prospects. Asia was our largest trading partner at the time, and most importantly, Japan was critical to our ongoing growth and success.

Businesses in that region were legendary for being slow to warm to new relationships, but once established, they were for life. They were also tenacious negotiators. They looked at the big picture, the long game. While most North American companies thought of long-term strategies in three to five years, the Japanese thought in decades or even centuries. It was an interesting contrast to the business world I was familiar with, which was commodity-driven and very short-term in scope.

Naively, I thought I was ready for this new experience. I had planned to go with a senior executive of an Asian airline. He had an intimate knowledge of the customs and local scene in East Asia. He offered to join me to ensure my success and support some of our largest joint customers. I couldn't have picked a better person to accompany me on this trip.

After weeks of planning, we met at the business lounge in the Chicago O'Hare Airport and discussed the trip at length before our flight to Narita International Airport. When we went to board the plane, my traveling companion was denied entry. His passport had expired. While it was a very embarrassing situation for him, I realized I was heading to Japan without the comfort of an experienced and well-respected business leader coming with me.

As I sat in my seat on the 747, I considered how I would navigate the travel required, arrange for local support on the ground, and approach each of the customer meetings without formal introductions to ensure I respected proper local protocols and traditions.

To be fair, I was blessed with a very thorough Executive Assistant. With her help, I was on top of my itinerary and the customary gift-giving to show respect for each level of authority in the room. In those days, I needed to have a concrete plan without the cell phones and the conveniences we have today. Between the thirteen-hour time zone change and slow communication, it wasn't easy to ask for help if needed.

Once in Tokyo, I tried to sleep. You would think it would be easy after a trip of that length, but it wasn't. Back then, you could still smoke on Asian-bound flights. As a non-smoker, no matter where you sat on the plane, you came off those flights craving fresh air to feel back to normal. To complicate matters, it felt like I was in a time warp. After a short three-hour sleep, I got up at 1:00am and headed to the largest seafood market in the world, Tsukiji Market, to watch the Tuna auction. Over the course of a couple of hours, thousands of fish were traded using a unique dialect found only at the market. It was fascinating to experience it firsthand.

Later that day, I explored downtown Tokyo, searching for the building where I would have my first meeting. Tokyo is a tough city to navigate, especially with little to no sleep. Once I found the spot, I entered an impressive office tower and made my way up to the top floor. Pretty amazing for a seafood company. In fact, the multinational business I was visiting owned not just the company but also the building and filled up most of the floors.

I was greeted by a smartly dressed hostess and shown to a boardroom, which could seat about twelve comfortably. While admiring the stunning view of Tokyo, the office door opened precisely when the meeting was to start, and a lineup of eight very well-dressed executives marched into the room. When I say they marched, it was more of a choreographed walk, unlike anything I had seen before. They all wore identical dark blue suits and looked straight out of the TV show Mad Men.

I stood up, and as each one, the most junior to the most senior, walked toward me to welcome me, they bowed, and we exchanged cards. I respectfully bowed back and handed them each a small gift, with the most prestigious given to their elderly Chairman. I learned afterward that the act of bowing also should reflect the position of the person, so the higher the official, the deeper the bow. Every culture has its nuances and understanding them not only shows respect but also a higher level of care to those you meet.

The meeting started, and instead of getting down to business, they wanted to talk about my personal background. I was used to those questions in social situations, but it was unusual in such a formal and unfamiliar setting. The conversation then quickly shifted to their interest in our company's philosophy, strategy, and our greater purpose. I was not properly prepared for this type of deep conversation. Sure, I was able to speak to the current market, our features and benefits, but to the greater purpose of the organization, I was unsure.

I felt outnumbered, but more importantly, I felt wholly

unprepared. Looking back, I can see that I was an inexperienced twenty-nine-year-old, but that alone is no excuse. I tried my best to wing it and hope for the best. But as my close friend, Randy Zupanski, an outstanding leader in the hospitality industry, has since told me, hope is not a strategy. I left the meeting feeling like I had let my organization down. I was totally out of my element. After all, I was just a seafood salesman from Atlantic Canada.

Only nine of us might have known how unprepared I was, so I decided to learn from it and move on. I forced myself to look into the metaphorical mirror and find a way to prepare for the unexpected. I needed to anticipate some high-level or complex questions that may be asked next time. There were many next times. Fortunately, I never felt unprepared again.

We all represent the companies we work for and understanding the why of an organization (their strategies, long-term goals, or value proposition) and being able to explain it is as relevant today as back then. As today's generations have more accessible education, broader access to information, and a keener interest in corporate intent, it may continue to grow in relevance.

Several months later, on a visit back to Japan, the Chairman invited me to golf at the Osaka Club. The course was impressive, but since I was not yet a seasoned golfer, I did not fully appreciate it then. I would love the chance to play there again, although the score would not likely be different.

The experience was very memorable, a full day that included being fitted for a custom-made golf outfit, breakfast while waiting, nine holes, and a break for a tea service in a garden too beautiful to describe. Another nine holes, then into the hot springs to relax before a lengthy dinner. While playing, I had a caddie for the first time. Wearing traditional Japanese attire and speaking no English, she would smile, hand me a club, and bow her head. I would lower my head and accept whatever she gave to me.

On one of the last holes, I decided to ask for another club. I remember wanting a seven iron, and she passed me a three iron. I politely declined and handed it back. She stopped smiling. I still thought I knew better, so I settled on a six-iron. She handed me back my three. Still smiling at the elderly caddie, I asked again for my six. As if looking for some higher intervention, she looked skyward and passed back my three. I thought, "Wow. She's tougher than the Chairman". So, I conceded, and I took the offered club. Facing the course, I gazed at the fairway and the steep mountainous decline beyond. I hit my ball, which flew over the cliff and disappeared forever into the abyss. Clearly, she was right, and it likely wouldn't have reached the ridge with any shot.

After the game, the Chairman and I talked as we climbed down to the natural hot springs. I searched for an opportunity to tell him I had felt unprepared when we first met, but learned from the experience. I believe my willingness to admit my mistake and share my growth changed and deepened our relationship. From then, we became friends, and he would speak to me about his early life and learnings.

When preparing for an important meeting, it is critical to frame and understand the outcomes you want. Be it a sales or leadership-driven discussion, having measurable goals can make the difference between success and failure. When you know the desired results, you can ensure you are appropriately prepared for the steps to reach them.

As a leader, knowing your organization's why and how to articulate it has become vital to attract and retain employees.

Today's employees seek employers who have passion and purpose. They want to be part of something meaningful that gives them something to believe in. All employees should understand and be able to identify their company's purpose. As a leader, you must ensure the message is ingrained, well understood and there is buy-in to the vision.

Key Takeaway

Preparedness should be well beyond the topics of any meeting. A leader must prepare for the discussion to go in different and unplanned directions, and ultimately, you need to understand the end goal you wish to achieve from the meeting and the why.

Secondly, never doubt your caddie. Better yet, be willing to accept advice from those that know more than you.

Chapter 7

Saying Yes

Taking Calculated Risks

Do you know your personal risk tolerance? What even is personal risk tolerance? Simply put, it is the amount of risk you allow yourself to take on. These risks can range from starting a new role or something more substantial, like an industry change or relocation. Knowing your personal risk tolerance is relevant to anyone pursuing a leadership career as it speaks to the limitations you might be putting on your own growth or success. Are you all in? Halfway in? Or worse, are you just there?

Over time, how we view our ownership over our growth and development has changed. Some people may suggest it is a generational shift. I would wager it likely is not. In recent years, I have heard many comments like, "I wish to develop and grow into higher levels of leadership, but I am really only interested in this role or that one", or "I would like it within a timeline that works for me", or "I really only have an interest in specific assignments". When looking at high performers, the largest difference I have noticed over time is that very few are open to relocation or significant change despite seeking personal development and growth.

It is fair to decide against a significant change at one point or another. After all, we all control our life paths. Yet, the potential for success exists there more often than not. If you think your risk tolerance has nothing to do with your career's direction, you could sell yourself short.

Being a child of the 1960s, I grew up during a different era. Business boomed. When young adults graduated from high school, they had the ability to choose from a myriad of career paths without secondary education. Many from my generation, and the ones before, would stay in the same field or job for their entire life. My father did. They also worked for companies and in industries that typically moved employees around. Banking and financial institutions, insurance agencies and the military are a few examples that thrived on movement through their ranks and across the country. It was quite common to have new neighbors and coworkers due to this type of relocation.

When I started in the food industry, I believed that considering roles in other sectors and being willing to move across cities and provinces would be the way to advance. So, when those opportunities came, Kathy and I discussed them, and for the most part, said yes for the rest of my career. We were extreme by today's standards, becoming prairie tumbleweeds as we blew back and forth across the country. What a journey and incredible life we have had because of it.

As amazing as it was, it wasn't easy. Every new opportunity meant saying goodbye to those around us whom we came to know and care for, but it gave us a chance to meet more people. Not all decisions to go were easy, either. Some locations we were asked to go to, well, were not our first choice. We balked at several great roles in Ontario due to concerns about traffic, smog and our perceptions based on hundreds of trips in and out of the Greater Toronto Area, but when we finally went, living there was the complete opposite of what we feared. We loved it. For every move, we learned all places could hold opportunities if you are open to them. Like the old idiom says, "Don't judge a book by its cover".

The world feels much smaller these days because people are constantly connected through technology. Our collective survival is wrapped up in it, keeping up with our ever-evolving personal and business needs. The ability to work remotely from anywhere in the world is changing the business landscape. For instance, if communication technology did not exist, the recent COVID-19 pandemic would have looked and functioned much differently. However, it could be detrimental if we close our minds to the possibility of relocation as a way to advance, grow and find fulfillment in our careers. Numerous relocations are less likely in the current climate as companies look to move employees far less than they did years ago. Yet, even one move may seem out of reach as part of some career plans. By using those standards, anyone willing to consider any magnitude of relocation will have the upper hand in advancement.

For most, acceptance of risk is dependent on your ability to adapt to change. Risk, by nature, is about taking a chance, but inevitably, it means change. For those limiting their horizon in any way, consider broadening your range and make it known to your leader. Since the pandemic, companies have seen sizable migrations of employees leave the workforce, and the search for great talent and leadership will continue to grow in need and importance.

Key Takeaway

Assess your long-term career strategy and let your boss or employers know how flexible you are to take on new roles and challenges. Ensure they know the type of roles you are looking for but be open to potential changes presented to you. Increasing your personal risk tolerance may open up a new world of possibilities. Find ways to show you are the right person for leadership opportunities, then watch them come your way.

Earning the Right to Lead

Chapter 8

Investing Time

Getting to Know Your Fellow Employees

One of the greatest investments you can make as a leader is getting to know the people you work with as coworkers and people. This time together builds trust and shows that you care for them beyond the needs of the business. People want to know you care for them as individuals. When you get to know the people you work with, you can better react to their needs or wants and be more empathetic and understanding when life issues occur.

Spending time allows you to see where their passions lie, if they aspire to bigger things, see their careers heading in different directions, or see themselves as future leaders. The more time you take to understand and know your coworkers or direct reports, gives you the latitude to ask what their dreams and aspirations are. Employees who feel guarded or intimidated by you are far less likely to be honest about their weaknesses or ask for help. Getting to know each other and being willing to discuss your own concerns, imperfections, or areas of improvement will allow others to see you as genuine and can lead to deeper discussions about professional and personal development.

Some choose to hide or be unaware of their talents, so you will need to build relationships that enable you to dig deeper to find them and help them shine. Some individuals may not see themselves as future leaders, yet they may be some of the best informal leaders in the organization. Identifying your employees' talents and inherent leadership traits is an essential skill of an organization's leadership team. There is no more satisfying accomplishment than identifying someone's underlying talents and developing them into great leaders beyond what they thought they were capable of. Outside of the pursuit of leadership, socializing also provides an opportunity to understand where other interests and talents might be hiding. We may start our careers heading in one direction, but the path can take a lot of twists and turns. These detours can be confusing when finding where our true talents lie.

A conversation I had with a seasoned top salesperson illustrates these concepts. We met over coffee and chatted about his lengthy work in sales. He told me he felt his career went differently than he had hoped. While he was a high performer in sales, he believed he would have got more satisfaction out of an operational role. This salesperson thought his success meant he would not be considered for other opportunities so late in his career. We agreed to discuss it again in a couple of months, and when we met again, he was offered a chance to transition into operational leadership. It was apparent that his sales and leadership qualities were transferrable and helped him attain the new role. More importantly, when this leader retired, his primary feeling of accomplishment came from finding the conviction to make such a profound change late in the game and finding success there.

The ability to walk up to any employee and start a conversation about their family, hobbies, or weekend plans develops an informal opportunity to listen and hear about how people feel and their concerns. The higher you go in leadership, the more important these deepened internal networks become. You can start one person at a time, and the earlier you begin, the better. It is a wonderful way to learn what others know that you do not. And it provides space for staff to share what they think could be improved, how teams could perform better, and how to stop obsolescence.

As people, we have more in common than not. I always felt at ease speaking with every person in my organization, no matter what position they held. This approach was not only good for business, it was also good for the soul. Their perspective and lives are just as important as those in leadership, and they can be just as ingrained in the business as you are. Employees may know a customer or a vendor personally and be better positioned to suggest how to improve those relationships. In my experience, some of the best cultural changes came from employees who were comfortable enough to speak freely about improving their organization.

Key Takeaway

There is no greater investment in time than getting to know people. Understanding your employees' qualities can lead them to take on more prominent roles beyond what they see as possible. Harnessing the informal network with your employees opens possibilities in hundreds of directions.

Chapter 9

Accountability

Knowing It's Not What You Say, It's What You Do

When I think back to my initial days as a leader, I often shared many things I planned, intended, or dreamed of doing. Unfortunately, my follow-up actions and execution of those plans were sometimes well below my stated intentions. I did not plan to fail, but I failed to follow through on what was said. People listen to what you say, look to you to provide vision, guidance, and insight into where the organization is heading. Both your leader and the team you lead will expect you to do what you say, so it may seem obvious to refrain from saying things you do not plan on doing. However, that is easier said than done. As leaders, we are part of many conversations. We want to ensure those around us understand that we have a vision and a plan. Ultimately, people will judge you on what you do more than what you say. Your actions, achievements, and results will more accurately show the type of leader you are.

Early on, at times, I would state my intention to deal with challenges but would not follow up. I told employees we would hit a target without a real plan on how to do so, and even more problematic, tell employees I would get back to them and not follow up. I sometimes made bold statements with the hope that things would just work out. But remember, hope is not something you can hang your hat on.

We all, leaders and employees, make statements of intent every day. As the saying goes, "If you're going to talk the talk, you better walk the walk". It is crucial to live up to what you say. Whether you rise or fail will be based on your ability to execute your commitments. That is not to suggest you under-promise and over-perform, but rather, think about what you're committing to and how employees could react. If you make bold plans, changes or speeches, be prepared to follow through on them. Things can change, that is business, but you must understand the expectations you have set. What happens if you make constant plans that you miss or fail to follow up on? Faith and trust in you will decline. People will be less likely to listen to what you say and are less likely to believe you are steering the company in the right direction. If you constantly act on what you say, you will be seen as a leader that holds yourself and those around you accountable.

Accountability is one of the key traits of a successful leader. People believe in and follow those who show accountability. When leaders start to separate what they say from their real intent or actions, things can go off the rails. There are many politicians who exemplify this idea. Ultimately, most people do want to be accountable for their actions and can tell the difference when others are not.

Think back to your past organizational leaders. Can you remember a time when leaders took ownership of their actions and were accountable to those around them? Results felt like magic since accountability at all levels creates unstoppable momentum. The opposite occurs when leaders are not held to their word and actions; results will stall and suffer.

To be fair, all organizations face external factors or things outside of their control. Yet, real leadership occurs when challenges are met with accountability and honoring your commitments. As part of the responsibility you carry, a leader must commit to setting and meeting those expectations.

Key Takeaway

When stating your intentions and plans as a leader, you must be prepared to meet those expectations and follow through on what you say. Hold yourself and others accountable by executing what you promise.

Chapter 10

Decision-Making

Conviction and the Element of Trust

I was fortunate early on to have leaders with strong conviction and trust in their team. They put others first and knew their success was based on the greater group achieving their goals. They were soft-spoken, listened well, intuitively saw challenges before they unfolded, and planned to act accordingly. Over the years, you will encounter many leaders with very different management styles, and each will achieve very different results. As mentioned in the previous chapter, we all react and determine the value of leaders on what they do rather than what they say, so living to this speaks to their authenticity.

Trustworthy people show strength in their decision-making, an open and flexible mind, and sincerity in what they say and do. Think of these exchanges between a leader and an employee as a bank account, a concept made popular by Stephen R. Covey in his book *The 7 Habits of Highly Effective People*. Each positive interaction deposits credit into your account. If you build up enough credit, through being trustworthy, honest, candid, and genuine, people around you will allow a withdrawal when you make a mistake. If you do not have enough credit built with people, you will struggle in arrears, like a real bank account. Leaders withdrawing credits they have not earned will struggle to keep their position. Those around you will call back your loan and simply stop supporting you.

As leaders, we are generally part of a hierarchy within our organizations. This means that, at times, you will be given a directive to take a position or provide direction to your team on an issue when you don't personally agree or support the direction. Your role as leader is to execute on what has been asked of you. It is an awkward position to be in, having to advocate for a vision or direction without being 100% bought-in. You need to be able to do this, and be decisive, to successfully perform your role. It's hard to do, and it can test your senses about who you are and what you stand for, but you need to be able to resolve these issues to lead with conviction.

I remember a time in the early 2000s when the company I worked for was planning to make adjustments to their bonus structure. While it appeared to have significant flaws in the reworked plan, the feeling was it could still be tweaked over time to get to the right place. I was not bought-in and pushed hard to get it 100% perfect. But as we know, perfect can be subjective, and it can often get in the way of being good enough to proceed. While I was able to get a minor concession before proceeding, it was still very hard to accept and roll it out. I felt it would be a disincentive to the impacted employees. Nonetheless, I needed to support the change wholly. If not, it would be hard to expect others to do so. As things go, the plan did what it was expected to do, and worked out to be the right direction to take. It was a good lesson to push back when you feel you need to, but there can be no confusion once the go button is pushed.

Indecision is born from indecisiveness. Weak or poorly thought out decisions create missteps and often do not end well. It is a ton of energy and work to get your team, or the greater organization, to be fully aligned and move forward on a decision. You never really can get 100% buy-in on any decision. There will be a percentage that are all in, some that are on the fence, hopefully not a picketed one, and others that cannot or will not agree, no matter what you do or say. So, with that in mind, consider a leader without strong conviction in their decisions. If conviction is not there, or indecision leads to countless corrections, employee support will be lost. The more time you spend heading in unclear directions, the less effective your final decisions will be. These successes or failures will have a cumulative effect on the level of support your team gives over time. This is why you need to know what path you want to take and effectively steer the organization there. Your ability and confidence in strong decision-making will ensure your staff will readily follow.

All that said, we are still human. Part of being a leader is being able to acknowledge when you have made a mistake or need to change directions. Correct your course and explain why the change is needed. A willingness to be open and genuine through successful and failed decisions will garner support and trust from your team.

These concepts remind me of a story. One night, a US Naval Destroyer approached a light off the coast of Nova Scotia. The captain on the bridge demanded several times that the source of the light change course. Each time, the source of the light responded, "Sir, we are unable to change. Please correct your heading." Very frustrated, the captain of the ship said, "No. We are a US Destroyer. You need to change yours!" The other party finally responded, "This is the Cape Island Lighthouse. Your call!" As a smart leader, you must be able to admit when you are wrong and acknowledge when it's time to change direction.

Key Takeaway

Having strong, trusting relationships with your employees allows you the latitude to make better decisions. Trust is foundational to everything in your organization. Nothing can be built, and no sustainable success will be realized without it.

Chapter 11

Team Chemistry
Building Winning Teams

There are tons of books on leadership that focus on—get ready for it—the leader. Wow, I guess that makes sense, right? Yet, successful organizations only achieve great results if they have strong teams with the right chemistry. Any good leader will tell you their success is built on, and as a result of, the people they surround themselves with. I believe it wholeheartedly. My greatest successes as a leader came from the talent and chemistry of my teams, not from me. Yes, a leader plays a part, but it would be a small percentage compared to the rest of the group.

This will be more apparent during times of adversity, when team dynamics are stretched and challenged in ways that don't show up in normal day-to-day conditions. One such example I reflect on is, during the final two years of my career, and in the middle of a pandemic which had devastating effects on the food service industry, we were also hit with a flood that shut off Vancouver from the rest of the province and country for over a month. Our division thrived through these extraordinary events for one reason; team chemistry. We were there for one another, we leaned into each other's strengths, and picked each other up during times of weaknesses. Simply put, we had each other's backs and could not be knocked off our mission to succeed, no matter what came at us.

A team's success is not based solely on ability. The most important aspect of any team is their collective chemistry. One of my daughters is a high school chemistry teacher, and she would likely find a better scientific explanation on the subject than me. However, this is less science and more human dynamics. From what I know about organizational chemistry, when human components fit perfectly, they can create positive reactions when brought together. As the leader, the key is finding the combination of talents, personalities and roles to produce the most favorable results for your organization.

These are massive decisions, as each team member needs strengths to achieve positive outcomes. Humans are imperfect, so finding people who fit together well will be difficult. When staffing your team, talent alone is not the most critical component. How often have you seen sports teams or businesses loaded with talent but function poorly together? Many teams have been stacked with all-stars but cannot ever seem to secure a win or championship. The human element forges complications no matter how well you plan, so be purposeful, not experimental.

Consider these points when building your winning team:

- Hire diversity with varied talents.
- Seek those that have differing strengths from others on the team.
- Find people with different abilities or experiences than you.

- Consider as part of your hiring process, using predictive personality tests for the team.
- Actively engage current team members in the hiring process for new members.
- Take a slow and methodical approach to all those joining your team.
- Understand where the imbalances in the team's chemistry are and actively address them.
- Candor within the team needs to be continuously high.
- Everyone is equally accountable.
- As a leader, you need to promote constant feedback loops between all team members.
- Once hired, let leaders lead.

I have been part of a few dysfunctional teams over the years. Getting a team to exactly the right place is like winning a relay race. Repeating it year over year is like finding a unicorn.

Having a high functioning team will start with the leader. You can either spend your time refining the best team or resolving the organizational fall out if you do not. I have seen teams with imbalanced chemistry, lacked candor, conviction and accountability, dismissed issues as they arose, and numerous other dysfunctions. It often boiled down to a lack of trust within the team. Regrettably, we are living in a world of diminishing trust. Our trust in media, government, institutions like banks, and new technologies have the human race on edge. It takes a long time to build trust and only seconds to lose, thus building and maintaining it takes constant work. If your team lacks chemistry or key components, trust will be at risk and nearly impossible to maintain. It is not easy, and even if you inherited a team, you have to start with what you have.

People struggle with having difficult conversations, so it can be very tough to get the wheels back on the bus if they are broken. However, the team will, at best, continue to limp along as long as they stay broken. You will never achieve the results you seek with an ineffective team, so it is up to leadership to deal with. My approach has been to start candid conversations with the entire team, outlining concerns as clearly as possible. Work on team development directly, with the assistance of others in the organization, or consult experts outside the organization if necessary. Lastly, make quick decisions on personnel changes when you know it is needed. Dragging your feet on tough decisions that affect your team is a sign of weak leadership. Your team will appreciate your proactive and strong approach if it gets them back on track.

Key Takeaway

Team chemistry is more important for achieving success than any one individual's strengths.

Chapter 12

Kindness

Showing Some Every Day

It has been said that kindness is the single most important leadership trait. If that is true, then why do many leaders struggle with it? Do leaders find it difficult to show kindness because they believe it shows weakness? Society has wired us to be ultra-competitive with "only the tough survive", nonsense. While working for a corporation many moons ago, I had a senior Vice President whose favorite saying was, "let the big dog eat first, and we are the big dog". Cringe-worthy stuff.

The bravado from some leaders paints a picture that the harder and tougher we are, the more we will win. You can see that show up when you look at some political leaders worldwide. That could be laughable if it were not so sad. Competition can be healthy, but overly competitive attitudes can create destructive behaviors. If your board or senior leadership team acts or speaks with excessive bravado and competitiveness, would it establish a culture where leaders express kindness? Likely not.

We all lead hectic lives, ones where the pace continues to

quicken significantly. In many cases, technologies meant to help us communicate have accelerated the speed of correspondence, but perhaps not our ability to deal with it. Attachment to our devices has disconnected many from critical human interactions. Our ability to cloak behind a wall of technology has beaten kindness out of so many people. It seems like our humanity has taken a back seat through the difficult years of the pandemic. Between the transitions to working away from colleagues (while successful at meeting employees' desired lifestyles and diverse needs) and the technology wall, organizational culture has been altered. Depending on the nature of an organization's industry, more damage could be done than we realize. Getting this genie back in a bottle, if possible, will not happen overnight. Where and how do we begin?

Let's start with the simple things, like the giving of time. There is no more special commodity than time; it is always moving forward and is non-renewable. We seldom appreciate its movement until we look back and understand what is now behind us. With that said, giving it to those around you is valuable. Freely sharing your time tends to be most valued by those who believe it is kind of you to offer it when received.

There's also the old basics of please and thank you, holding a door open, offering assistance to someone, or giving up your seat to someone in need. I still see glimpses of hope, but particularly in larger cities, kindness and humanity seem to be all but gone. It is so easy to start a request with please and finish with a simple thank you, but why don't we use them anymore?

The real question becomes: How do we instill courtesy and kindness into our leaders? Employees stay with employers due to their relationships with their bosses or fellow employees. Therefore, it would seem that relationships where kindness is apparent would be more successful than those without it. Beyond daily greetings and conversation, leaders who take time to connect with others through all types of correspondence are beneficial. Handwritten cards still offer a sincere and often profound impact because very few people take the time to do them. Speaking of which, where have all the Christmas cards gone?

Giving can involve just about anything, like things that show we care, flowers, or items that lift spirits that have always been used and welcomed by those who receive them. But giving can also be listening, providing support through challenging situations, recognizing causes like charities, volunteering, teaching, mentoring, or sticking up for those unable to defend themselves.

It is the little gestures you do that, at that time, do not seem significant but are the right thing to do. These gestures bind us together and make relationships more than interactional. Care and kindness can provoke strong emotions, maybe more so in today's world where divisiveness seems all too common. You may not know the positive impact this has on others, but it certainly does. Companies often offer time off, pay in lieu, or other things to show their appreciation to employees, but then will miss gratitude for simple and smaller achievements. Employees may expect the big things, but often they remember the small things just as much.

Demonstrating kindness to new employees during their early days with you and the organization is important. It is good to institutionalize the practice within your entire employee community. Do you remember how intimidating it can be when you first started with a new organization? Employees who are greeted with smiles, warm welcomes, and immediate support will assimilate and be retained much longer than ones that do not. And don't forget, encouragement can be a powerful form of kindness. Instilling these values in those around you, especially new hires, allows them to see the endless possibilities of success, if not within their current grasp. Using supportive words of encouragement tell people you care and are willing to stand behind them when times get tough. As well, take time to recognize acts of kindness and the encouragement of others every day. Pointing them out will help others see the benefits too.

The busier we all become, the more kindness can become an afterthought. Timing can play a big role as there may be a need to show compassion and sincerity in that moment or the impact will be lessened after the fact. I sometimes woke up in the middle of the night and thought I missed doing the right thing in the moment. Remember, taking the time to check in with someone or following up will always be worth it.

Key Takeaway

Employees stay with organizations mostly due to their relationships. Our kindness needs to become an intuitive activity in our daily lives. The more we do it, the easier it will become. The culture of an organization will rise to the level of kindness shown by the people within it.

Chapter 13

Listening

Don't Do All the Talking

Most of our first impressions of leadership are someone speaking to us. Perhaps it is from a teacher instructing a class, at work when the boss addresses you, or from our parents' guidance at home. We develop a very early sense of leaders, where they tend to do a lot of the talking. There are certainly millions of reasons why leaders speak; it's important that they do. Yet, our sense of what leadership means can be skewed by the belief that you must be the one doing the talking in order to lead. Ironically, most great leaders talk much less than they listen.

In my initial phases of leadership, I tended to talk too much, likely full of self-importance. I thought what I had to say was more important than everyone else. I could feel myself interrupting others for years to get my point across. It took a long time and some exposure to some great leaders to see what was truly important; listening to what was actually being said and really hearing it.

Our greatest opportunity to learn is through listening to others. Why, then, do many leaders feel it is necessary to continually talk and not stop to hear what is being said? The more you listen to every source, opinion, comment, or even a rant from your employee, the more likely you will make better, well-informed decisions. Excess ego can play a role in why some leaders cannot find the balance between speaking their thoughts and listening to the information others may provide to help.

It can be particularly tough for young leaders to take the time to listen. They tend to want to be seen as knowing what is right, what to do, and show they are in charge. A very old hierarchy view of leadership, in my opinion. Most of us struggle with this notion from time to time, sometimes more than we care to admit. But, as my oldest daughter often pointed out to me, "That is a you problem!"

Over time, I was exposed to some incredible leaders who knew how to gather great intel and truly listened. Initially, I thought of these traits as weaknesses. How could they not know all the answers? How naïve and, frankly, immature. I later understood they were exceptionally patient and knew the value of learning through tremendous listening skills. Perhaps best demonstrated by David Barber, a leader I had the pleasure of working with for several years. David had some of the best listening skills of anyone I was fortunate to be led by. He was a professional accountant by trade and spent most of his career as a senior executive in finance, human resources, and leadership of national food distribution organizations. David showed infinite patience, but ultimately, his genuine interest in hearing what others had to say influenced and informed his decision-making. These skills demonstrated an ability to ask great questions, to appropriately react to what was said, and to ask deeper follow-up questions. He often repeated back what he heard to ensure understanding and then asked for clarity.

Even with a willingness to listen, communication barriers can still create obstacles that we need to overcome. Once upon a time, while sitting in a hotel room in Luxembourg, I received a message via the front desk about a distribution issue I had in East Asia that required immediate follow-up. This involved finding a way to get multiple people on the phone, only to then have a number of delicate conversations. At that time, you needed to use the hotel operator to make basic calls. More complicated ones could be very frustrating and required a lot of patience. I picked up the phone in my room and asked the German-speaking operator to contact an Asian airline office at the John F. Kennedy International Airport in Queens, New York. The person that picked up after several minutes of trying to get through had a very strong Bronx accent. I explained the issue, and they agreed to reach out to the importer in Seoul. When the Korean-based importer picked up, we spoke for several minutes and agreed he should get his superior on the phone. They spoke even less English, but after another ten minutes of what was fairly elevated discussion, they called the freight forwarding agent they were using, who happened to speak no English at all. Several more minutes of back-and-forth dialogue took place before a resolution was reached. In all, about one hour of communication had taken place, but much of it required repeating more than once. When I checked out, my hotel bill included the Canadian equivalent of the cost of the call that took place earlier that morning. It was just over $700.00. Try explaining that on your expenses in 1990.

The saying, "we have two ears and only one mouth", is a good reminder of the ratio of listening to speaking we should aim for as leaders. Admittedly, it takes time to understand this and even more time to apply it. Reflecting on it now, I suspect there were great opportunities I missed out on by not applying this thinking sooner.

As leaders, we are faced with employees who are upset and want to let you know about it. None of us tend to enjoy conflict. It's not the part of leadership we look forward to. Occasionally, you can be distracted or busy with other aspects of the business, so pushing off the conversation becomes easy. However, to ensure your organization's culture remains strong, you must find the time and prioritize listening, no matter who it is or what it is about.

In my earlier years as an Operations Manager, I had an incident where an employee, that I had a low degree of trust with, spoke to me about some concerning activity in our warehouse. He suggested that our warehouse and transportation department were a conduit for drug-related gang activity. Initially, I felt the statement was deflecting a separate issue I had with this person. It was so random, and I dismissed the news because it seemed implausible. While the source seemed dubious, the statement was serious enough to warrant a deeper dive. Over the coming days, it became apparent that this issue warranted police action and surveillance installation. Shortly after that, the organization had a huge problem on their hands. This was not an isolated experience, either. I had more situations throughout my career that turned out to be larger than what appeared at face value. As a leader, it is essential to be open-minded enough to investigate issues, no matter how trivial they seem. Listening to my employee's complaint and looking past whatever else might have clouded my judgment would have helped me take action quicker and potentially mend a relationship.

Once, as an exercise on communication, my organization's leadership took four groups of ten people and gave the first-person specific details in a story about two paragraphs long. In turn, we gave each person two minutes to convey the story to the next group member until all ten heard the story. The last person to listen to the details would share the message. That message was nowhere near the original one communicated. Each time we did this, the story took on a life of its own. This experiment is no different than many discussions taking place each day. It is an excellent lesson in understanding the critical nature of communication flow and how we listen or, more accurately, don't.

To help you along your journey to become an incredible listener, here are some opportunities to improve your skills:

- One-to-One: Have meetings with every leader in the organization and have them lead the agenda and discussions.
- Reviews: Share any written documentation beforehand with both parties to allow more time for open discussions.
- Town Hall / All Employee Meetings: Hold employee meetings regularly and use most of the time for answering questions instead of giving presentations.
- Informal Group Sessions: Host a meeting or group discussion over a meal. Breaking bread together is a social way to have others open up.
- Drop-Ins: Informally drop by offices, departments or visit with people you work with when possible.
- Open Door Policy (and mean it): Make sure you tell people that you welcome feedback, ideas, and

visits. Move your office to a place where there is greater visibility and accessibility for employees.

- Have a Different Perspective: Ask others to present at or lead meetings so you have time to listen and observe.

Key Takeaway

Take time every day to actively listen. Great leaders hear their employees and reflect before speaking.

Chapter 14

Common Purpose

Harnessing the Power of Many

Many organizations struggle with silos, where each department and its people tend to be solely or predominantly focused on their own areas of responsibility. Silos emphasize one department or group's needs over other departments, coworkers, or organizations. Often, culture surveys show silos as the most common concern. When employees feel siloed, it keeps them from seeing the benefits of organization or cross-departmental cooperation. Silos can place both visible and invisible barriers to success. Worst case, it can result in a complete breakdown in culture, and the company's results can suffer.

From my earliest days to my retirement, I spoke with employees who said their department works well, but that others were creating issues and holding them back. Silos will create friction in all companies from time to time. Some friction will help stretch flexibility between departments, creating healthy competitive spirits, but other times, not so much.

Corporate strategy planning tends to have charts and lists of responsibilities by department to achieve the desired outcome. But this type of thinking may set the organization up to work in or continue to work in silos. Instead, when developing organizational strategies, focus on a common purpose to drive the business forward. Organizations that use common purpose as a key strategic focus will win more in the long run. Those who use that strategy to focus on their customers will win even more. Furthermore, establishing key performance indicators that measure a company's customer performance allows buy-in from all employees, and the company will sustain greater momentum over time.

Using another analogy, you may find an orchestra with the greatest musicians, but they do not sound as good as they could. Alternatively, you could have a sports team full of superstars, but they never win the big games. These high-performance individuals may never reach their full potential in silos. Organizations can find themselves in difficult situations if their leaders only lean on a couple of key contributors or one department to carry the weight of achieving the company's expectations or bottom line. Achieving sustainable results will come from teams that work well together, sharing the business burdens equally. Simply looking great on paper won't cut it.

I know a leader who really believes in the power of cross-departmental training in organizations. This leader understands that cross-training is an effective way to lessen the impact of silos by temporarily moving talent from department to department. Doing this lets you share a department's strengths and impart a message that every person and department is important. While cross-training or job sharing is helpful to an individual's development, perhaps the best outcome is for them to gain an appreciation for what others in the business do. Empathy from understanding creates an environment that is tough to break. It becomes leadership's task to make cross-departmental change attractive to their employees and show them that the outcomes are worth the effort.

How often, where, and the kind of team meetings you hold can make a significant difference to your success as an organization and help drive a common purpose. Time spent together should be treated as a sacred trust between your employees or leaders, with the utmost care, as you are using up valuable resources to do much more than get together. These days, companies are struggling with meeting culture by gathering too often without a set purpose, overloading tight agendas, and running overtime. It is critical to respect everyone's time and find the right balance. To change things up, you could try a new venue, move the meeting to where the work is being completed, or find a way to keep the discussion as brief as possible. Lastly, remember to evoke fun in your meetings. A good laugh together will develop a positive atmosphere where momentum can thrive.

From leadership's perspective, the key purpose of a meeting is to gain collective understanding, foster collaboration, and confirm the group's buy-in. Information sharing is better suited to other communication methods like email, newsletters, and less formal conversations. Ultimately, the power, productivity, and success of your team will start with you.

Key Takeaway

Leading a team with a shared purpose is always far more significant than where individual talents will take you. As leaders, we must foster a culture that creates and lives up to those standards.

What You Will Come To Understand

Chapter 15

Expertise

Learning Which Metrics Drive Your Business

At the beginning of my career, my business knowledge was limited. If you are also in a new leadership position, you might find yourself in a management role where you may not fully understand the drivers of what makes your business successful.

Moving through my career, I found that many leaders, including myself, needed to learn how business metrics, like key performance indicators (KPIs), are calculated and measured. Even if you understand the principles of what it takes to be successful, like sales growth or the bottom line, if you do not know how they are measured, you can put yourself in a vulnerable position.

In my case, it showed up early, as I spent more time on developing relationships than focusing on metrics. I remember being asked about things like our cost to price, or whether markup percentages were based on sell price or cost. As I found out, this is not a part of leadership that you can "fake it until you make it". I can recall not knowing and then guessing the answer. Leaders will not always have all the information on every topic, but risk will be compounded if you make assumptions based on incorrect data. Ultimately, not taking the time to learn the details could have and probably did lose the company money.

Leaders require a deep understanding of their organization's KPIs. Seems like common sense, but surprisingly, many leaders don't take the time to learn them, inside and out. An interesting exercise to try is to ask people to explain their understanding of some of your KPIs, and you may quickly see that not everyone interprets them correctly. Leaders can help everyone get on the same page by seeing where the gaps in understanding are.

If you are responsible for setting up business metrics for your employees, be cautious about inadvertently getting in the way of the organization's goals. When leaders measure and reward their employees using their results, it can cause a myopic view of your business. Focusing only on the numbers will prevent innovation and exploration of new ideas and opportunities. Employees who think their KPIs will be negatively impacted may not pursue the idea because of the performance risk.

Every so often, leaders should review their business metrics to confirm whether they still line up with the company's goals. At one point, I worked for an organization that felt they had a great bonus program. Like many other companies, they rewarded employees and leaders based on dollar sales growth, profit, and other typical sales KPIs, as these areas carried the largest percentage of payout. Where the disconnect came from was that the program was based in US dollars, since that was their primary market. People would be either over-rewarded or under-rewarded, depending on the currency fluctuation. Rewards from KPIs are most effective when they are consistent and aligned with the business's goals, so revisiting these programs will ensure their effectiveness over time.

You could suggest the most important key performance indicator is your bottom line, but I have seen companies put just as much emphasis on top-line growth or other metrics. Publicly traded companies likely argue valuation is a better KPI than bottom line. Ultimately, metrics should be about measuring your success. From the ground floor to the boardroom, you need to align your employees with what is important, how it is being measured, and create programs that meet the organization and their workers' needs.

Key Takeaway

As a leader, you must understand the drivers and metrics of your business, inside and out. That knowledge is power and will ensure you can explain the how and why to staff. Unfortunately, there are no shortcuts, and it will reflect poorly on you if others know them, and you do not.

Chapter 16

Crisis Management

Using Calmness and Humor to Lead

When I retired from my last leadership role, even though I was excited to spend more time with family and friends and travel, leaving it behind was tough. My successor told me they thought we had not only survived the pandemic's challenges, as well as the province's most historical natural disasters, but excelled through them because I brought calmness and humor to work every day. As a leader, I believed that no matter what was happening around us, what kind of day I was having, or what issues I was dealing with, a little levity, fun, and stability was the key to enduring any hardship. This was especially true on the darkest days we faced as a team, when we needed to make difficult decisions, or didn't see a way through the situation. Of course, I appreciated this feedback, but it also gave me pause to reflect on the amount of stress the team had withstood over the past few years. Some of those days were unforgiving, likely some of the toughest times many of us might face in our careers.

My natural response during stressful periods is to remain calm. I believe I developed this strength during my years as a referee. As an example, I refereed a senior game where an unhinged player came in from the blue line and kicked the goalie in the chest. The players on the ice had a nuclear meltdown, others left the bench, and things were really getting ugly. In that moment, I needed to survey what was happening while remaining collected. It was a challenge to keep the adrenaline down while the chaos flooded everyone's veins in the arena. Thankfully, in that situation, I was able to gain back control by reinforcing with the coaches that they needed to get a handle on their teams. If you allow emotion to get the best of you, you can make quick or poor decisions or even create bigger problems. If it happens, it is very difficult to rein it back in.

We all have natural tendencies when it comes to how we respond to others. In fact, many personality assessment tools are available to help provide an accurate snapshot of how we show up in our natural state or even under stress. These tools can effectively demonstrate the areas where we have personal strengths and areas where we need improvement.

Calmness, or an ability to be composed, collected, and stable, are vital leadership traits in a crisis. Employees will often look at how their leader reacts to a situation, so if the leader remains collected, they will be more likely to follow your cue. If you are losing your mind, or even showing stress cracks, don't expect those around you to keep calm. Your reaction to a challenge or crisis as a leader will be the most scrutinized by the people around you. If they see their leader expressing that the sky is falling, they will start to consider if effective leadership will be present when things get rough.

When we think of great leaders throughout history, many stayed calm in the face of danger, adversity, or defeat. The British are famous for their steadfast and resolute statement, "keep calm and carry on". But how do you keep calm or return to an unemotional place when you have allowed the situation to get the better of you? Breathing techniques can work. Slow, deep breaths allow your heart rate to slow. Or perhaps you can take a quick time out by stepping away to regain your composure. Get some fresh air, or get a good night's sleep, if possible; both can make a difference in your ability to gain perspective. Finally, try thinking of multiple solutions to the issue. Reflecting beyond your initial reaction or quickest solution may help you find a better way forward. It is natural for your mind to have a flight, fight, or freeze response when in crisis mode, so remember to slow it down.

Admittedly, I can remember a time when my initial reaction to a possible crisis was not serene, and I needed to find my way back to the right place. On a flight from San Francisco to Calgary, I watched two very tall State Troopers enter the plane and ask over the intercom for a passenger with my name to identify himself. I think the customers and fellow employee I was with on this business trip could sense my fear in that moment. I remember wondering why California police would be looking for me. It was only a few weeks after the events of September 11th, and everyone traveling on planes or working in airports was on high alert. No one looked relaxed, especially the officers at the front of the aircraft.

As I put my hand up, the troopers came down the aisle, asked me to stand up, and exit the plane with them. I had no idea what was happening, and my heart rate was high enough that I wondered if everyone could hear it pounding. I thought, my god, had someone put something in my luggage? When I asked one of the officers what was going on, they said, "Sir, we are not at liberty to say. Please come with us. We are taking you to meet with airport officials."

Once in a small room, several airport security personnel explained that I had breached airport security and created a security hold on flights. *WHAT?* My mind raced. How could this possibly be? I was not at all calm. Then, I thought about the moment the group had boarded the flight. We had been asked to transfer from Air Canada to a United route after our flight was canceled—another fallout in the immediate days after the September 11th tragedy. I remembered the group was transported through the basement of the airport and went through a temporary gate on the ground level. A security guard waved for some of us to come forward, and when I did, she said something to the extent of "get going". We were running late, and the plane was holding take off for us. I took her statement as I was good to board. Maybe it was a mistake on my part, but I certainly hadn't meant to breach security.

I asked the security people to find the agent who boarded us and see if she would remember her frantically waving at us to get going. After what felt like an eternity, she appeared. The troopers and security personnel questioned her out of earshot. She looked around them, nodded yes, and then gave me a disappointed look. It seems they heard enough, so they came toward me and said, "Mr. Robertson, you need to take more care next time you travel to the United States. We take our security very seriously, and you need to as well." It turned out to be a great example of how a simple mistake in understanding could have huge negative implications.

After being escorted back to my plane, I took a long walk of shame down the aisle to where my customers and co-worker were anxiously waiting. The flight was now 45 minutes late, and everyone on the plane was unhappy. These were not friendly times in the sky, after all. I was relieved we were on way our home, but my heart still buzzed until I was back in Canada. With the hundreds of flights I have taken since, I pay a lot more attention to what people say, and thankfully, I have not caused any further security issues or delays.

Beyond remaining calm, my other coping skill is humor. I have a dry sense of humor and learned I could defuse a situation with a well-placed comment. I have been part of many organizations that grew quickly, and some that did not. The successful businesses were led by people who constantly pushed their teams to learn and grow, while alleviating stress when they could.

Have you heard the baseball phrase "holding their bats too tight"? You might use it if a player or a team cannot seem to get a hit in a playoff game. The same analogy can be applied to business. Employees or teams under stress (like tight timelines, or big sales targets to reach) can get tunnel vision and not see the bigger picture. We do the same things over and over but expect different results. Some call it analysis paralysis. These are all signs that they could be holding their bats too tight, and the higher the stress, the stronger the grip. So, how do you help ease stress that is creating a performance issue?

Humor tends to be a common coping mechanism for people, and it works. People respond well to humor in just about every circumstance, but in a crisis, you need to evaluate the situation and use your judgment in any attempt to lighten things up. If you are able to transition the mood to be more positive, your team are more likely to think and perform better.

Some leaders benefit from stepping back and focusing less on the goal or result. If you can pause or relax enough in stressful moments, you have a better chance of successfully changing your trajectory, if needed. Finding ways to have fun will help you do that. Coaches in sports have higher degrees of success when they keep the mood light with their players. Everyone performs differently, and some forms of motivation work better than others. Yet, demanding leadership, with no joy or fun in their approach, might yield only short-term success. Like with an autocracy, this self-serving approach may result in something other than the type of support you need for long-term effectiveness.

I have worked for a few leaders throughout my career that had the personality of a wet sock. It's tough going through life without levity or leisure, but it's hell for the staff. Lighten up. For most of us, the work we do won't bring world peace or cure cancer.

During my last year with a company back east, we had a strike at our facility. As things can go in a strike, emotions flared and were fueled by busloads of union supporters that drove in from around the province. No doubt stoked by a drink or two, the crowd could easily turn into a nasty mob. The boss had decided to invest in a water cannon as the last beacon of defense. Live on the news, we watched a security guard in a yellow hard hat holding the line. He yelled at the nice folks outside the fence, alerting them that he was prepared to unleash a torrent of water on anyone that breached the wall.

The angry crowd advanced, and the fence fell over. The security guard turned on the cannon. Turns out, it was about as strong as a water pick, and the water barely made it out of the business end of the cannon. Before complete mayhem ensued, the owner turned to us and said, "I can pee harder than that cannon." The room erupted in laughter. It certainly showed us that even in the midst of a riot, there is room to laugh and not let this bring us down. Most importantly, when things get tense, make sure you allow yourself a little space and time to think beyond the current issue.

Someone I recently worked with in food distribution said, "We are not saving lives, we are selling fries." Meaning, many things are not worth getting your knickers in a knot. Sometimes, we build things up in our head to be a much bigger deal than it likely will be, especially when it is something negative. As humans, it is in our nature to be cautious and fear the unknown. However, if you're able to focus on the positive, it will allow you to balance more possibilities. When we set our expectations higher, we are more likely to have better outcomes.

Right up to my last day before retirement, I found a way to inject humor in some facet of the work we did. Keeping it light worked well for my team. Just days before the pandemic started, I arrived in a puffy penguin suit while one of our leaders presented a leadership class on the book, *Our Iceberg is Melting* (John Kotter/Holger Rathgeber, Portfolio), a story about a colony of Penguins and how they dealt with a pending disaster. Little did we know that less than a week later, the beginning of a two-year global trauma would unfold. Truly ironic, but that presentation set the tone for how we would deal with the pandemic every day, with humor and calmness.

Of course, this is not rocket-science, but a great reminder for us to reflect on how we approach our days. Go to your office with a positive attitude and share it. Instill fun into the working day. We often forget people like to have fun at work too. An organization is more likely to retain happy employees. It goes a long way if your employee smiles on the way home when remembering something that made them laugh, instead of another mundane day. Work can be a boring routine, so leaders who find purposeful ways to inject fun into work will retain talent. If in doubt, remember the saying, "people laugh all the way to the bank".

Key Takeaway

Remaining calm in a crisis will help your employees focus and navigate uncertain times. Leaders who allow their minds to relax can stay positive and are more creative in finding solutions. Take time to smile, laugh, and reflect in difficult times. And finally, find a way to inject fun and humor into your work and relationship with your team, if and when appropriate.

Chapter 17

Leading Sales Teams
Why Sales Leadership Is Different

One of my career's greatest joys has been leading some incredible sales teams—both with one of Canada's largest food distribution companies and one of Canada's top seafood exporters. Top-tier sales organizations are highly energetic, constantly in motion, and require exceptional people to maintain and grow extraordinary customer relationships. Internal bonds in sales teams come naturally from the group's shared experiences and the rise and fall of business. They are no more important than any other person you lead, but sales teams can be more complex than other departments you might manage.

Salespeople are who they are, and we love them for it. They can be lone wolves and very independent. Occasionally called road warriors, they may live out of suitcases for much of their week. They tend to be prominent, type-A personalities. There is a reason we can easily picture the stereotype of this role in our heads. However, as abrasive as some of those individual traits can be, those people will also knock down doors for you, handle objections, ask for the business, keep going back for another shot, and drive your business forward. The challenge is finding sales stars who can do all those things exceptionally well.

One commonality all sales teams share is that they are at the front end of the wedge with customers. They are the face of the organization, and as such, you will require a team that is wired to serve and be available whenever and wherever your customers need them. Salespeople will always be the first to hear when issues arise and as such carry a lot of weight on their shoulders. Organizations and leaders can help carry that weight by having policies and support in place that remove obstacles instead of adding to them.

As an example, I have seen simple issues arise in an organization when Finance put policies in place that, while seemingly prudent and well-intended, became a great disincentive to the sales team. In one case, a per diem was put in place that was reasonable for employees that might travel infrequently or for part of the day but was so limiting it only covered the cost of a steady diet of fast food for anyone who was on the road consistently. The question needed to be asked of those who put the policy in place; would you travel every day under those circumstances? The answer was no, so the policy was adjusted to be more in line for the sales team to maintain healthy eating habits while traveling.

People in sales are likely extroverted, competitive, and often thrive on recognition. Many want to dominate the leaderboards and see how they compare with others. The top sales performers thrive on it, while others further down the ranks may use it as motivation to get to the top. Part of recognition and acknowledgment is to celebrate wins. People come to work to succeed at what they do and hear that what they do matters, so celebrating achievements with the entire team should be a part of the organization's overall culture. Leadership will do their organization a disservice if wins aren't recognized when they occur because they give up a chance to enjoy success together. With salespeople being the closest to the customer "fire", they may feel responsible for any business or customer lost. For some sales reps, they take it as personally as a break-up since they are the primary contact in the relationship. Because of the win-and-lose nature of sales, acknowledging wins will reinforce and validate their value to the business and balance the reality of losses when they occur.

As a sales team leader, it will benefit you to understand that time is money for this group. Sales meetings, or any activity that takes them away from serving their customers, should be well thought through. Finding balance in dealing with required sales reporting, long-term strategy and planning, and even technical issues will be a fine line—they need to be completed, so be candid about what is expected. Clear direction will prevent ambiguity and create less follow-up. If the sales team is bogged down with the administrative needs of customer maintenance, consider whether another department can take on processes like accounts receivable or pricing.

Sales leaders need to be flexible with salespeople who may be pulled in opposing directions, like relationship management versus internal reporting. Salespeople will go where the money is. Gaining or keeping a customer's business will be the bigger priority. As a sales leader, a flexible approach will help to show your own adaptability in managing each member of the team to get the maximum results.

Key Takeaway

Sales will be the major driver of business growth, so sales leaders must find the right team dynamics and balanced management approach to get the most out of their salespeople.

Chapter 18

Feedback

Understanding It Is Gold

I once worked with someone who often said he looked forward to his upcoming review. Funny, since he did not like feedback and hated change. Of course, he was joking, but it might not be far from how some people actually feel.

Everyone enjoys receiving compliments and hearing positive things about themselves. Yet, as a leader, the real value you can provide anyone with is candid feedback on performance and areas of improvement. As mentioned in a previous chapter, it is vital that a leader has enough trust established with their employees, so there is mutual respect during the interaction.

Giving constructive feedback is not always easy. No one looks forward to hearing that they are not doing their best or meeting their employer's standards. However, real growth comes from both understanding areas that need development and recognizing achievements and progress. If you tell an employee they are doing everything right, where is the opportunity for growth? Conversely, it can be incredibly unmotivating if you only point out when and where they are underperforming. So, take time to provide continual feedback, and ensure you touch on both the good and bad in a reasonable manner and time frame.

Giving proper and helpful feedback takes work. Beyond the informal conversations, leaders must first schedule enough time in an office to meet face-to-face. In some cases, a location change may be needed to reflect the type of feedback you give. Generally, I held most meetings in my office, although some employees may be more comfortable in their own space or a neutral location inside or outside the office building.

Regardless of the location, keep your attention focused on the person you are meeting. Here are some tips to give productive, concise, and effective performance feedback:

- Do not take calls or allow external interruptions.
- Write down what you wish to cover, especially if there is a specific order to the information you need to cover.
- Try to stay on point, and do not ad-lib. Going off script could create new issues that will not help a difficult conversation.
- Remain as calm, unemotional, open, and candid as possible.
- Allow the feedback recipient to take notes and leave ample time to ask questions or clarify what they heard.
- Encourage two-way dialogue and have them repeat points back to you if needed.

- Keep the conversation professional. The main goal is to ensure that the feedback is understood and actionable where necessary.

Lastly, leaders must ensure that the feedback recipient is confident that their privacy will be respected. This can be challenging to navigate, as it may be necessary to approach others in the organization about the topic. Yet, keeping confidentiality when soliciting information is critical for maintaining trust and credibility, so proceed with utmost caution.

Even as a leader, you may receive unexpected feedback, but remember that all feedback is valuable, even if it is not what you want to hear. Feedback can and will find you in many ways if you are open to it. Appreciate the time someone takes to give you this information and thank them for it in a manner appropriate to the moment. Refraining from taking comments or feedback in isolation is a good practice. If you add them to what you already understand based on past experiences and feedback you have received, then you can build a more complete picture. People are motivated to say things for many reasons. Whether it be praise or criticism, the person giving the feedback can occasionally be biased or tainted. Is the information coming directly from the source, or is it potential hearsay or a rumor? If you are unsure, consider how trustworthy the source is. Did you seek their input, or was it given voluntarily? Whatever the reason, all feedback is just information. Use it in the best way possible.

Leaders may seek more information from the source or others to comprehend and validate the merits of the feedback they receive. During this process, be sensitive to the parties who provided it by acknowledging they gave it, but also consider that sharing it has left you with questions or gaps in details, and you plan to inquire about them.

Key Takeaway

Feedback is a sacred gift. Respect and appreciate when it is given to you, and when you are providing feedback, treat the interactions with candor, care, and compassion.

Chapter 19

Empathy

Having "The Talk"

The first time you need to let someone go from your organization, and every time after, will be some of the most traumatic experiences you will face as a leader. Those types of events can cause immense stress for both parties. The facts leading up to you sitting in a room, facing someone, and having an uncomfortable discussion do not really matter. However, properly preparing for the termination meeting is critical to being the leader they need you to be. The reason you are meeting should never be a surprise to the person sitting across from you.

In my opinion, there is a right way and a wrong way to proceed with these situations. Most organizations, particularly larger ones, will involve their human resource department. Still, as the leader of the person being released, you should be fully engaged in the preparation and be the one to begin and lead the conversation.

The most important quality a leader must display in these meetings is empathy. As difficult as that conversation will be for you, it may be one of the toughest moments for the employee being let go. Even if their termination is a for-cause dismissal, everyone is human and makes mistakes, even "good" people.

During my time in leadership, I have had the misfortune of taking part in numerous dismissals over the years. Looking back, I wish I had this advice to get through those challenging conversations:

- Be empathetic and kind about what is happening to the employee.
- Be well prepared. Read any needed documents prior to the meeting to ensure they are correct and plan how the discussion should proceed.
- Hold the meeting in a private area to avoid any disruptions. If possible, book it in a location that allows the person to exit with limited staff interactions.
- If a member of the Human Resources team is not present, arrange for at least one other company representative to be there.
- Have tissue available. Never assume how people will react.
- Be brief and direct when commenting on why you are there. Documentation will cover any supporting information, and giving excessive details or extraneous comments may create further issues.
- After you speak, leave time for the person to acknowledge what happened, decompress, and express anything they wish to say.

I remember watching the former New Zealand Prime Minister, Jacinda Ardern, speak on leadership qualities during stressful times. By all accounts, she was an incredible leader and led her country through three major disasters: a devastating earthquake, a mass shooting, and the pandemic. During her speech, she expressed that the most essential traits a leader needs to possess are kindness and empathy. It is hard to argue against that.

Through being empathetic and compassionate in your approach during the termination process, the person you are dismissing will be in a better place to understand the decision and likely reduce the emotional distress they experience. It also may help the employee start processing the steps toward acceptance and allow them to move forward with dignity.

As I retired, I received notes from colleagues and employees over the years. Surprisingly, some congratulations and well wishes came from people I terminated. Despite what had happened, it was humbling that they still took time to reach out. It was critical that I ensured the person across from me wasn't belittled and that I cared about what they were going through. "The Talk" will always differ, depending on the circumstances, but all employees must be shown fairness and respect. If ever in doubt, consider how you would want to be treated if you were let go.

Beyond these difficult talks, empathy is necessary in all facets of leadership. It is how we understand the thoughts and feelings of people around us, and it also contributes to our own self-awareness. For instance, you may put off speaking with someone regarding a mistake or decision if they had a personal emergency to a more appropriate time. Effective and empathetic leaders find a way to balance the business's needs with the needs of their employees.

Key Takeaway

When you need to terminate someone, treat them the same way you would want to be treated. Everyone deserves kindness and empathy, especially in tough conversations.

Chapter 20

Your Brand

Who You Are as a Leader

Leadership can be very challenging, and it is not getting any easier. Nowadays, companies and their leadership are under a lot of pressure as people adjust to a world event that left them exhausted, beaten down, and forever changed. Many have chosen to leave their jobs or industries, now known as the "Great Resignation". On top of that, millions of baby boomers, like myself, are exiting the corporate workforce. Economically and socially, things do not seem great out there. Now, in this altered world, it has become increasingly difficult to lead. Acquiring and maintaining momentum in the current environment requires extraordinary leadership and a strong connection with employees.

People have a lot going on, both in their personal life and at work. Their relationships with their leaders and company have become increasingly strained. Under this increased pressure, your leadership style (your brand) is more critical than ever. How do they see you? How would they describe you and your interactions with them? What do you offer them?

First, and foremost, the results you and your team achieve have a significant impact on your brand. Your track record will speak to your ability to get things done. Effective leaders should be equal parts results-oriented and culturally driven. Too much focus in either direction will sacrifice results or culture, and neither should be an afterthought. Sure, metrics will speak for themselves, but how does your team and others view you as a cultural fit? Maybe your team tells you because you ask. Or perhaps you use talent optimization tools like predictive index testing, or 360-degree performance reviews to get a cross-section of feedback from people you interact with or lead. It helps if you are self-aware and try not to take anything personally. Even so, results will rely on understanding how your employees see you.

Leadership is a delicate balance of so many countless factors. Many attributes that we cover in this book are positioned along a sliding scale between two opposing sides.

For instance, your leadership brand will find balance between being selfless or selfish. From a selfless standpoint, leaders demonstrate this trait by being available to their team and customers 24 hours a day, 365 days a year. Leadership requires a level of dedication and availability that shows you can be there for support, take calls, and handle anything that comes your way. Yet, you need to find some ways to be selfish to find balance. Take time with your family, rest appropriately, continue to educate yourself, cross-train emerging talent, and find ways to enjoy life. Finding this balance is more challenging for some than others. You will be pulled in both directions, so you may lose sight of what each means. How can you be all things to both sides of the pendulum?

Your style of leadership may come down to who you are

and how well you find your equilibrium, which, in turn, establishes your brand. Stay too long on one side of the spectrum and you could be known as a workaholic or a micro manager. This type of leader may be seen as disempowering, uncooperative, and overbearing. On the other side, you could be missing the big picture or small details or never be willing to get involved or get your hands dirty. This leadership style will seem aloof, disengaged, and show a lack of accountability with their team. Again, your style will have consequences and affect your brand, in both good ways and bad.

There are a myriad of traits that can be put on this scale. Reflect on how you think you fall between these opposing characteristics.

Servant.........Autocratic
Empowering.........Dominating
Bombastic.........Reserved
Approachable.........Stand-offish
Intense.........Relaxed
Intimidating.........Approachable

Can you naturally identify where you fit and adjust behaviors to find the right mix? Identifying may come easily, but changing our behaviors is more difficult to do. Our personalities as adults tend to become hard wired, and we are not always aware of how our behaviors affect our interactions. Developing the art of compromise, flexibility, and adapting your approach will always be of value in leadership and life. We all have a compass that points us to almost every belief we hold. Therefore, changing can be tricky since your genuine self is your north star, and often, your natural tendencies will overrule where you are consciously choosing to go.

The leader you are depends on the person you are, and it's healthy and wise to continually assess yourself and your path. Over time, your brand will determine your success and ability to grow into higher levels of leadership. You likely have notable strengths as a leader and have areas that require work to improve. Other people's assumptions about you may not always be accurate or fair, but generally, it is in human nature to analyze and assess others. If senior level leaders, or those in a position of influence, do not see you as a good fit for leadership because of their assumptions, it can affect your ability to get ahead and place limits on it. The question becomes, how do you change the brand they see you as?

Firstly, you must understand the leadership position and identify how the decision makers see possible gaps and barriers to you getting that position. Are they fair and reasonable? If not, work on a plan with realistic timelines to address them. Get constant feedback on your progress and confirm their concerns are actioned. Understanding where your career development gaps are can also help to keep out of a branded box. Whether you believe the barriers in front of you are fair or just, it is key that you determine a strategy to reinvent your brand in order to overcome them.

You may also benefit from job shadowing or cross-training where the gaps in your experience or expertise are. Demonstrating a commitment to continual learning and growth can combat concerns and lay them to rest. Considering a lateral move, or taking a step down, could show your ability to thrive in an area that may be beyond your role's reach.

Your brand and who you are as a person are more on display now than they ever have been. Social media platforms provide an ability to connect and share our thoughts and lives at an increasing rate. While there are many positive aspects of social technologies, a leader must be cautious about what is shared online. When you are in a position of authority and have others looking to you to lead, your reach also grows. Be diligent when deciding what and how much of your opinions and personal life to post online. And it isn't just about what you post. Associating with concerning ideas, companies, or people can negatively impact your brand and reputation. While I am not a social media expert, I know the more you allow yourself to be exposed, the greater the risk to your brand. At the end of the day, you make the best decisions for you, so proceed with caution, but trust your judgment.

Key Takeaway

Your brand is you. Understanding how you are perceived will allow you to make conscious decisions and corrections to your brand of leadership. Finding and maintaining a balanced approach to your style will ensure your success and longevity.

Chapter 21

Curiosity

Seeking Relentless Understanding

Nearing the end of my career, I took on the President role of a large foodservice distributor. As I flew into a new city, I thought about the upcoming introduction to my new team. It was to be a sort of reveal party. I knew the reason I took this role was circumstantial. The senior team underwent significant change and needed a different leader from outside their ranks. It was time for a new direction.

This division had an impressive history, which they worked hard to earn. They had been one of North America's best food distribution companies for years, but their market had matured, and business flattened over the past few years. While the regional opportunities seemed promising, the optimism appeared low. I wondered what I could offer in my short opening remarks with the group. What wisdom could I share that would set the tone for their new start and shifting focus? And how and why was their business suffering?

Sitting on the plane, I jotted down some words we all know and use; communication, self-driven, ownership, and accountability. All good ones, but nothing new. Nothing that we could build something fresh on. I then considered, what don't I know? What about this team, their new people, their chemistry (or lack thereof), their strategy, and their market are keeping them up at night? What is stressing them out? Or better yet, what aren't they worried about? My questioning led me down numerous paths during that flight, but all were driven by constant curiosity.

It struck me. That's it! I needed to learn about where the leaders were with relentless curiosity. Has the team lost their zest to learn? Have they been empowered to push the business, or were they asked to stand on the sidelines, watching the parade go by? Having an interest in asking any and all of the questions that needed to be answered was a way for me to learn their system and to help them find a path forward. If we did not know the answer to things that were critical to the business, then the team would surely flounder. Its either be curious or be complacent. Complacency and indifference will squash out any ability to be open to new ideas.

Once I arrived at my new office, I spent time getting to know the team. After getting acquainted, I told them that I felt the business was stagnant because they had a very mature, well-tenured group, and it seemed they had lost their way. Their spark, mojo, and curiosity were gone. While there were many reasons this was the case, the group agreed to address these concerns over the coming months.

Curiosity is fundamental to life, business, growth, and especially, leadership. You can usually see who has a zest for knowledge and who doesn't. Those who are driven to continue learning will excel at far faster rates. For example, a salesperson who asks informed and intelligent probing questions will yield better results than one who is solely focused on cultivating relationships. If you can do both of those things well, you will win the majority of the customer's business over time.

Of course, being curious and asking great questions is an entry-level requirement for better understanding. More importantly, it sets you up for what can come next. It gives you something to action. Because of this, leaders must be as curious as everyone else, if not more. You cannot coast as a leader. If you are not asking the right questions to your direct team, your employees, your customers, and your vendors, you are doomed to lackluster performance at best.

Do you accept answers at their face value? Do you follow up for deeper understanding or just to clarify? Do you ask others for answers to the same questions? Do you look for answers that are different from your own opinion? Answering these questions may give you a barometer from which you can assess your own level of curiosity. The higher your interest and attention, the more information you will possess to make well-informed decisions.

Think back to a situation where you have made a decision on gut instinct or on impulse. I would guess that you did not take the time to ask the questions you needed to ask or get the information needed to make a thorough decision. Giving yourself the time to stop and reflect on what questions need to be asked to attain the desired outcome can bring laser-like focus on how to get the answers. Sounds simple because it is. Relentless curiosity can help provide more possible outcomes, and the more paths you see, the more you have the ability to choose the best option.

In our primary education, we learned the five Ws. Using these can provide perspective for framing up your questions.

The list below shows how you could apply them to being curious about your business.

- WHO: Who is involved? Who are the decision makers and stakeholders? Who supports this and who doesn't? Who can I ask about this? Who are the possible winners and losers in this scenario?
- WHEN: When does this need to be completed? When is the timing most critical and will things change based on it? When should I sleep on this decision? When should I move quickly before someone else does, or should I walk away because it is too quick to jump in?
- WHAT: What is the reason for this change? What questions still need to be asked? What is the expected outcome? What happens if this deal doesn't go through? What information do I need to pass on to others?
- WHERE: Where do we start? Where do we want to land? Where do we expect to change?
- WHY: Why did this happen?
- And as a bonus, HOW: How did we get here? How might this decision unfold? How much will this cost? How will it impact our bottom line? How will this decision impact my employees, customers, or team?

When I reflected on the time spent leading that organization, many successes pointed back to the first day. Establishing the importance of curiosity with senior leaders created an environment where:

- We became more self-aware.
- We asked better questions of others and ourselves.
- We asked for clarity when we did not understand.
- We started to reject the status quo.
- We began to challenge things we did not agree with.
- We secured and retained a lot more business.
- We made better strategic operational decisions based on better information.
- We drastically improved our results.

It was abundantly clear that our increased curiosity expanded our business in unexpected ways. We thought we knew there were opportunities, but until we stopped finding ways to be limited, we would never have found the level of success we did.

Key Takeaway

Asking the right questions leads to the right answers and decisions, and ultimately, better outcomes. Maintain constant curiosity. It is essential to your growth and success.

Chapter 22

Resiliency

Keep Moving Forward

As mentioned earlier in this book, nothing is insurmountable. Your ability to survive through anything is borne from your own resilience. History is full of stories of human resilience. Much has been said about how difficult these past few years of dealing with the pandemic and lockdowns were for people. We felt the effects of isolation, lack of connectivity and community, and an inability to move freely. Why is any of this relevant for business?

Many organizations, much like people, have dedicated a lot of time and resources toward dealing with their first global crisis. While many events in human history could be deemed worse, it was a test of resilience for us. Many businesses faced temporary closures, massive drops in sales and revenues, government restrictions or interventions, social changes, changes to employee expectations, lay-offs, restructures, bank foreclosures, bankruptcies, etc. How, as a leader, do you lead through times like that?

In some cases, many leaders had no choice but to face things head-on, day by day. Business owners also experienced the real possibility of losing their businesses. It became a matter of survival for owners and leaders to show resilience during those challenging times. One strategy was to shorten and redefine timeframes to what was realistic, manageable, and, hopefully, achievable. This allowed some companies to reset and refocus their resources. For others, it was a matter of finding a way to live another day, because once you throw in the towel, it's hard to go back. Businesses folded, and owners walked away to lessen the financial or even mental effects of the pandemic. Companies may still have yet to feel the full impact on their business, even now, three years later.

The worst of times can bring out the worst in people, but it can also bring out the best. Organizations worked to carry their employees through the darkest periods when their own futures were uncertain. Some companies showed that as stewards of their communities, they needed to honor the people who supported them, and many unspoken social commitments were kept in place. Conversely, a shortage of employees often meant the ones who stayed worked longer and stretched themselves thin to ensure their families and employer would survive.

From the events of the past few years, I've learned a key lesson in leadership. Your team should always have contingency plans and processes in place. Just because business is good now does not mean there will not be a point where it isn't. Beyond taking the time to develop emergency preparedness plans, how many companies review them regularly, test them, and adopt changes when needed? As 2020 showed, many companies did not have or execute them well. Resilience is not a substitute for a lack of preparedness. You cannot count on your team's or your own ability to wing it through a crisis. You cannot operate solely on hope that you have enough in the tank to get through an extended challenge. In those instances, you may have to rely more on luck than on good leadership. Never a good place to be.

Beyond building a contingency plan, an effective leader will ensure their employees are prepared by cross-training individuals and teams, ensuring audits yield strong results, correctly staffing based on business needs, carrying a diverse pool of staff with varied experience, and enforcing vacation policies and work-life balance. Well-rested and sufficiently cross-trained employees will better sustain an organization through a high-stress situation. If your team is overworked, confused, and running on fumes, expecting them to be resilient in an emergency is unrealistic.

To gauge your organization's resiliency, consider whether they have a corporate support mentality to have all-hands-on-deck when needed. Does the head office, national or regional support network step in to assist in a crisis, or are they often missing in action? Do you and your organization have a battle-room mentality that allows resources to be redeployed to the right areas or priorities? Is the company siloed to the extent that people will struggle to support each other? Are policies up to date and do they align with common sense when they need to be applied? Does your organization cut expenses in non-essential areas, thus leaving you vulnerable in a crisis where resilience is required?

As a leader, are you prepared to guide others in an emergency? Do you take time away from the stressors of work, or are you fully engaged 365 days a year? Do you have other personal issues that will allow stress to compound or seep in when you need resilience? Do you leave time to train, keep updated on things you should be, and hear new perspectives? As the leader, your resilience is paramount, as others will look to your energy level, commitment, and how you show up every day during a crisis.

Key Takeaway

Resilience is a combination of your inner strength, preparedness and practice. You need all three to survive and thrive.

Chapter 23

Enjoy Every Day

Taking Stock of Your Journey

As I reflect on what it takes to be a leader, I think of the commitments and sacrifices it requires. They can take a toll on you and your family. The best advice I received to combat this was to take time daily to enjoy the little things, the big and small wins, the upsides, and the new experiences. Our lives and careers are brief in the grand scheme of things. Finding a way to enjoy each day will balance the tough times and challenges and help reveal feelings of joy, satisfaction and accomplishment. If you hyper-focus on the function and performance of your role, you will quickly run your tank dry. Remember, to be a resilient leader, you must keep a full tank; it is your responsibility to find a way to do it.

In your leadership role, you will participate at a different level. You get to see things you would otherwise not see, like the development of your employees, the achievements you share together, and the results of a team. You will meet people that will have a profound impact on you as a leader and a person. Whenever possible, take a moment to reflect on the time and positive experiences you share together. In turn, you will become part of a larger business community as you continue to grow, share, and network with other leaders. Enjoy the benefits that this new community provides you by actively participating in industry or trade associations. Your leadership network could expand your reach with new customers or vendors as they travel across other companies, and they may develop into relationships that last a lifetime, like many of mine have.

Perhaps you will have an opportunity to travel more in your new role or relocate. While they both have their challenges, it also provides an opportunity to see places or things you would otherwise not have. I was very fortunate to have a lifetime of experiences that would fill many bucket lists as a benefit of business travel and relocation. Through those relationships perhaps you will also take some time to play a little golf, fish, dine, catch a game together, or share other experiences with your customers as I often was able to.

One of many special times enjoyed in my roles was to host customers at various moments over my career. It was something fulfilling, both business-wise and personally. What a great opportunity to really get to know one another. Many such events, even when well planned, went off the rails, which made them even more memorable.

I had a customer years ago, Steve from the Hawaiian Islands, who had never been off the Islands, expressed an interest in visiting our head office in Nova Scotia and doing some trout fishing. He had read about it in a sports journal, and it was something he always dreamed of. Over the next several months, a plan was put in place to bring him to the east coast.

After a lengthy journey and overnight flight into Halifax early that July, we headed down the coast of Nova Scotia for a couple hours and then turned onto a logging road for another forty minutes. The midday sun was getting very hot as we pulled up to our spot, although neither of us cared about the heat as the anticipation of a large trout on the end of our line was all that mattered. We thrashed into the thick woods, full of black flies and ticks, and made our way to the river. We talked about our lives, enjoyed some great fishing, and had a lot of laughs. For me, this was a trip done many times, but for Steve, it was a once in a lifetime experience and it was a thrill to see the happiness in his face. We had a great day, landing a number of Eastern Brook Trout with their beautiful white and blue spots along with their red bellies glistening in the sunlight. Even though Steve had traveled a long way to catch them, we were just as happy seeing them slip back into the dark pools they came from as we were when they first came to the surface for our flies.

Into the late evening twilight, we talked about great food dishes we had enjoyed and the meal we would have when we got back to Liscombe Lodge, a resort I had booked us into. Night was falling and as sad as we were to reel our lines in for the last time, we were really ready for a shower and that seafood feast I had been promising him.

As we made our way back from the river, we looked out of the now dark woods at my truck, which had a small glint of light coming from my headlights. We looked at each other, realizing this wasn't what we wanted to see. Neither of us wanted to ask the question, why is the light on in the truck? As I leaned into the cab and tried the ignition, it clicked but did not have enough enthusiasm to turn over. Oh no, it was now confirmed we were miles deep in the bowels of the Nova Scotia wilderness with no way out.

We thought about our limited options. Walking to the

highway was out of the question, so we resigned ourselves to a night in the truck with no seafood buffet. Steve had a great sense of humor, but even this must have tested it a bit, I thought. After a couple hours went by and just as we were settling enough to catch some uncomfortable sleep, miraculously we saw some headlights of another truck on the logging road. As the truck pulled up, the person indicated they were a forestry worker staying at a camp further inland and was now heading back to the highway. Luckily, we had jumper cables, so we were on our way to the lodge a couple minutes later. Once we got to the lodge, shortly after 1:00am, the only food available was from the vending machine in the form of chocolate bars which we readily ate.

Steve remembered that trip and our shared experience and often reminded me I still owed him a seafood dinner in humorous ways. That Christmas he sent some boxes of chocolate-covered macadamia nuts. When I called to thank him, he told me he got them from a vending machine.

Key Takeaway

Take time to enjoy your leadership role and the life it affords you.

Chapter 24

Letting Go

There's No Future in the Past

Do you hang on to things, your missteps, mistakes, poor results, not doing as well as expected, and many other issues that can haunt your mind? We are wired to be very competitive. Evolution of survival of the fittest still plays a part in our worlds every day. Yet, we need to find coping mechanisms when we don't have the successes in everything that we pursue. Hopefully, as leader, you will make many more good decisions than poor ones and enjoy more wins than losses, more successes than failures, but you will encounter both over time.

What is your reality when you aren't on the right side of these? Are you able to focus and look forward or do you dwell on them? If you find yourself in a stew over these things, you need to find ways to allow yourself better ways forward or it will hold you and your team back. Balancing the recognition of what has happened to what will happen next can leave the best of us on an emotional rollercoaster of second guessing with no stops in between. Setting realistic goals and then applying reasonable measurements against them on a regular basis can provide a way to keep your progress against your expectations in a more realistic place.

One of the favorite sayings I heard during my career was from Dean Noble. Dean is currently the Chief Operating Officer of one of North America's largest food service distributors and has held various senior executive roles as leader of Canadian and regional distribution companies. I worked with Dean over many years in several roles and consider him a close friend and a mentor. He is a Maritimer, a real people person, and has a very good sense of humor. We faced a lot of business challenges together. As my leader, I always appreciated that, no matter what the issue, he approached it with a positive, forward-looking attitude. Dean used a saying; "There's no future in the past". I love this, as it can fit into so many business scenarios. He often used it with me when I was focused on an issue that clearly was behind us and I couldn't impact. I think it was his way of saying let it go and get on with it.

Over my life and career, I've experienced lots of mistakes, missteps and things that could have been done better. When you're in a position that requires a lot of decisions, it's inevitable. Often though, I carried these issues beyond their shelf life, lost sleep, even impacted my health periodically. It would have been much better to let things go and move on, as these things can cause you to second guess or hesitate when making future decisions and certainly can cause you or others to lose confidence in you. Sometimes the tendency is to get so focused on the immediate issues that it can cause you not to keep priorities or look toward the future with the optimism it deserves. You need to. Take heart though, life is full of circumstance, and we will all struggle at some point to get through things, but it's a good reminder, get through it we will.

Thinking back, I laid some real eggs in my time. One such event, I put off and then forgot to register our fleet of vehicles in New Brunswick, which were due on April 1st, a Sunday. That night at exactly midnight, all of our vehicles that went past a scale were told to park, as they were no longer legal to drive. After a driver called me and woke me up to tell me what had happened, I started to call anyone that might be able to help. I got into contact with the government official who oversaw our region, and then the Provincial Transportation Minister, who was really happy to be woken up at 3:00am to be asked to provide temporary permission to get our many trucks back on the road, and our goods to market.

My intent, like all of us, was always to try to do the right things every day, to come to work and be successful. Life, however, often gets in the way of our intention and we don't have a script or manual to follow as we interact and make more complex decisions through our careers. I remember telling both our children we didn't have a definitive book on parenting. We made a lot of mistakes along the path, but it didn't keep them from becoming great adults. No matter, when we make mistakes, accept them as just that.

It's also the right philosophy when dealing with employees. We need to find a way to forgive and forget mistakes that our staff make. This is not to suggest we need to ignore mistakes, it's just that we need to recognize mistakes are normal and essential for all of us to learn from and do better. Overreacting or under-reacting to mistakes creates issues that either open the door for more to occur or causes employees to never take risks because they are too consumed with how you might respond.

Key Takeaway

Mistakes will be made. No one is correct in every decision they make. It's best to cut yourself and those around you the slack you or they need and find a way to deal with them. Make acknowledgments and corrections as best you can, and then put the mistake behind you. "There's no future in the past" really is a simple truth. If it's done, you can't change it, even if you wanted to.

Final Reflections

Leadership is hard work, and at times, the journey will seem daunting. Through developing a strong foundation, the challenges of leadership will seem more within your grasp and roles will become more fulfilling. While it has not been easy to summarize the qualities, characteristics, and behaviors of an effective and successful leader, I sincerely hope you are able to utilize the concepts in this book to guide you along your path and grow into the leader you wish to be. Leadership, like life, is to be experienced. Remember, there are no shortcuts.

Now that my career has come to its end, I look back on it with pride of accomplishment. As I have shown, it wouldn't have been possible without the incredible guidance and support I received along the way. The lessons learned have not only made me a better leader, but more importantly, a better person. I think of the naïve but hopeful young person I once was, and I wonder, what advice would I offer him today? The same advice I want to give you. Be confident. You can do whatever you put your mind, energy, and talents toward.

So, what kind of leader will you be? What foundation will you build upon to reach your goals? What legacy do you want to leave behind? While the journey is long and with immeasurable challenges, its rewards are many, and so worth it for those that do it well.

Enjoy the journey. I know I did.

Acknowledgments

I have been blessed with a career influenced profoundly and positively by others, and in writing this book, I hope to honor those mentioned here in sharing some of the journey we spent together. It's important to put back more than we are given.

I have received an outpouring of support while writing this book and I would like to take this opportunity to acknowledge them.

Thank you to my wife, Kathy, for supporting me through the many challenges and conflicts in my career with grace, understanding, and unwavering love. Thank you to my daughters, Kaleigh and Jenny, for accepting, albeit reluctantly, our continuous relocations. My leadership career and this book would not have been possible without your love.

An additional and special thank you to my daughter, Kaleigh, for her guidance with the development and editing of this book.

Thank you to Shane Kroetsch for providing technical and formatting support in the final push to complete this project.

To those that took the time to preview and provide feedback on the development of this book, you have my sincere gratitude. Thank you to my many friends and mentors, David Barber, Dean Noble, Frank Geier, Gary Seaman, Laurie Harding, Randy Zupanski, Ron Faithful, Chris Ramus, and others who inspired me to do better and helped me grow as a person.

To those people mentioned throughout the book and in my stories, I thank you for the inspiration, laughs, support, and guidance. I will continue to hold these memories dear.

Special thanks to Andrew Robertson for his valued feedback.

To you, the reader, I hope I have set you on a path to success. I wish you well on your journey to become an incredible leader.